Touchy Topics

Melvin Tinker

EP BOOKS
1st Floor Venture House, 6 Silver Court, Watchmead,
Welwyn Garden City, UK, AL7 1TS

web: http://www.epbooks.org

e-mail: sales@epbooks.org

EP Books are distributed in the USA by:
JPL Distribution
3741 Linden Avenue Southeast
Grand Rapids, MI 49548
E-mail: orders@jpldistribution.com
Tel: 877.683.6935

British Library Cataloguing in Publication Data available

ISBN 978-1-78397-179-4

Melvin Tinker has that unique ability to teach important ideas, make constructive arguments, all while entertaining with lively stories, examples, and lucid writing. I love all his books, including this highly relevant one on the topics that often occupy our conversations. This book is a must read!

Mark Lanier, Author of Christianity on Trial

Melvin Tinker is to be commended for his latest book. His purpose is to equip Christians to communicate the gospel in a culture that has forgotten God. His vision and voice is refreshing. Melvin Tinker is a man of Issachar. He understands the times in which we live.

Andrea Minichiello Williams
Chief Executive, Christian Concern

The touchy subjects in this excellent book are, in fact, the deep subjects of life. Finding answers to questions like the nature of God, his sovereign control in life, evil, and suffering, is what makes up a person's worldview. In this book, where faith is seeking understanding, these and other subjects are probed with care, sensitivity, and faithfulness to the truth of Scripture. Only God has a comprehensive knowledge of life but we can know enough of what is true for an understanding that is sufficient and satisfactory. This is what is spelled out for us in this very good book.

David F. Wells
Distinguished Research Professor, Gordon-Conwell Theological Seminary

Melvin Tinker has written a very helpful book that tackles head-on some of the most contentious issues facing Christians, both inside and outside the church. Concise without being simplistic, he engages deftly with contemporary culture and philosophy, and provides a biblical framework that will enable Christians to be more confident in their faith and equip them to be more effectively in evangelism and apologetics. Packed full of useful quotes, it will also be a good resource for preachers who want to ensure that they are addressing the questions that their congregations are asking.

John Stevens
National Director, Fellowship of Independent Evangelical Churches

To Heather with deepest gratitude for 40 wonderful years

Contents

Preface

In the West today it is generally assumed that faith and reason stand in opposition to each other or at least that the mind has very little to do with either commending or defending the Christian faith. In part this is due to the propaganda of the New Atheists. So we have Professor Richard Dawkins claiming that faith means, 'blind trust in the absence of evidence, even in the teeth of evidence.'[1] However, it may also be that in some cases the cap actually fits. There are varieties of Christianity which cosy up to the post-modern outlook whereby one is suspicious of claims to objective truth, resulting in a retreat into what is subjective and relative, 'My faith is as real as I feel—don't question, just believe.' Sometimes Christians have understandably drawn back from what they see as an over cerebral faith—where the finer points of doctrine are debated endlessly at the expense

---

1. Richard Dawkins, *The Selfish Gene* (Oxford University Press, 2006), p 198.

of love and obedience. There is also an increasing suspicion
in some evangelical circles towards apologetics, commending
the Christian faith in a reasoned way by means of biblical
engagement with the culture. As the late philosopher
Anthony Flew lamented over a generation ago, 'Belief cannot
argue with unbelief: It can only preach to it.'[2]

But wholesome, balanced Biblical Christianity would not go
to such extremes. I remember hearing Dr John Stott say that
the aim of the pastor is not to produce Christian 'tadpoles',
that is, creatures with large heads and under-developed
bodies. Nurturing a Christian mind and using it, is not a
form of rationalism—the sole use of reason, for there is at
least one other aspect of the mind which is just as vital for
the Christian and that is the use of the imagination, and both
are meant to be connected to the affections. This is loving
God with our mind as our Lord himself said, '"Love the Lord
your God with all your heart and with all your soul and with
all your mind". This is the first and greatest commandment.
And the second is like it: "Love your neighbour as yourself."'
(Matthew 22:35–39)

The purpose of this book is to encourage and enable
Christians to think through a wide range of subjects which
tend to be rather 'touchy' that is, they are contentious both
within and outside the church. Some are decidedly more
'touchy' than others, but all of them need to be worked
through with Scripture as our guide.

If Christians are going to be able to stand for their faith
in the increasingly bewildering market-place of ideas which
exists today, they themselves must be able to have at least

---

2. Anthony Flew, *God and Politics* (Hutchinson, 1966), p 9.

some grasp of these contentious subjects. Christianity by its very nature is not a 'retreat religion', withdrawing into a ghetto of pietism or mere proclamation at the expense of persuasion. As B. B. Warfield once remarked, the Christian faith 'stands out among all religions, therefore, as "the distinctly Apologetic religion."'[3]

It is hoped that this book will be of service in enabling believers to develop a way of thinking on such matters which will help us move towards fulfilling that great commandment of loving God with all our being—including our minds, and so be better placed to love our neighbours as ourselves.

I would like to thank Mark Lanier and the wonderful staff of the Lanier Theological Library for the use of this splendid facility in the writing of this book. I also wish to express my gratitude to the staff and congregation of St John, Newland, Hull, for their example in seeking to think 'Christianly', by having God's Word shape their outlook and practice. My thanks also go to Philip Tinker for checking the manuscript and making helpful comments. Finally, my heartfelt gratitude goes to my wife, Heather, who, as always, is my best and dearest friend and critic. This book is dedicated to her with inexpressible thanks for 40 years of faithful marriage in which she has encouraged me in my walk with Christ, ministry amongst his people and the raising of a Christian family—a privilege which is second to none.

Soli Deo Gloria

Melvin Tinker
The Lanier Theological Library, Houston, Texas, 2016

---

3. Benjamin B. Warfield, 'Introductory Note' in Francis R. Beattie, *A Treatise on Apologetics*, Vol 1 (The Presbyterian Committee of Publication, 1903), p 26.

1

Is God a Delusion?

In this chapter I want to consider a touchy topic which is one of the most common objections to Christian belief. It is one which is alive and kicking in the intellectual world, the media and probably held by many of our friends. It is based on a way of thinking which simply debunks the Christian faith and disallows many views Christians hold even to be expressed. Indeed, it is an approach which means that opponents of Christianity don't have to do any serious thinking at all. It is a strategy especially favoured by the advocates of 'Political Correctness'. I then want to take a look at how the Christian apologist, C. S. Lewis, deals with this objection both by way of imagination and by way of argumentation, first by looking at an episode in the Narnia stories, 'The Silver Chair' and then an essay he wrote in 1941. We shall see that his argument is as valid today as it was when it was first formulated.

First of all let me summarize the crude version of the way the objection we are going to think about works and then take a look at a couple of the more sophisticated versions of the argument by referring to the writings of Sigmund Freud and Richard Dawkins.

The argument in a nutshell

The crude version goes something like this: 'The reason you are a Christian is because your parents were Christian and you have been brought up in a so called "Christian country". Had you been born with different parents or maybe living in India, you wouldn't be a Christian at all, you would probably be a Hindu.' Or cruder still, 'The reason you are a Christian is because you are so pathetic you need an emotional crutch to lean upon'. This is in the same category of the man who dismisses his wife's objection to his excessive drinking by saying, 'You would think that—it is typical of a woman!' Do you see what is happening? It is being *assumed* that religious belief (or *any* belief for that matter), such as 'excessive drinking is bad for you'—is not supported by reason or evidence. Rather, it has some other 'cause'—the influence of parents in the case of the one, and a woman's mentality in the case of the other. Accordingly, belief is not simply explained, but *explained away*. You simply *assume* the person holding these views is wrong and then find an explanation as to *why* he holds such stupid and weird ideas. You don't argue, you assert: it is of the 'You *would* think that wouldn't you?' variety of debunking.

Now let's take a look at this in its more sophisticated form.

Freud's Dad

The classic instance of this debunking approach to religion is Sigmund Freud who tried to provide a psychoanalytical basis for the view of the German philosopher Ludwig von Feuerbach that God is nothing more than a projection of man. This is the way Feuerbach put it, 'Man—this is the mystery of religion—projects his being into objectivity, and then again makes himself an object to this projected image of himself thus converted into a subject ... God is the highest subjectivity of man abstracted from himself.'[1] In other words, there really is no God; he is simply a fancy of our imagination. The fact that the vast majority of humankind believes in a God is no evidence for his existence—it just tells us how sad humans are in needing to invent God. This turns on its head what the Bible teaches in the Book of Genesis that, 'man is made in God's image'. 'No', says Feuerbach, 'God is made in *our* image'.

Freud assumed this and then tried to explain *why* it was so.

In his book *'The Future of an Illusion'*, Freud wrote that religious beliefs are, 'illusions, fulfilments of the oldest, strongest, and most urgent wishes of mankind ... Thus the benevolent rule of the divine Providence allays our fears of the dangers of life'.[2] That is to say, primitive men realizing they lived in a dangerous world needed some kind of security that things will turn out alright. This is provided by the unwarranted belief there is a higher power who would help them make it through life. It is from here that we get the notion of 'wish fulfilment'. We only *wish* there to be a God otherwise we wouldn't be able to cope. And so, according to this supposition, people set about constructing religions.

---

1. Rodney Stark and Roger Finke, *Acts of Faith: Explaining the Human Side of Religion* (Berkeley: University of California Press, 2000), p 1.

2. Sigmund Freud, *The Future of an Illusion* (Penguin Great Ideas, 2008).

That may be OK for primitive people, but why do *modern* people feel the need for a God? This is where Freud sought to explain religion away in terms of *neuroses*. He wrote of 'the intimate connection between the father complex and belief in God' and stated how psychoanalysis shows 'that the personal god is logically nothing but an exalted father, and daily demonstrates to us how youthful persons lose their religious beliefs as soon as the authority father figure breaks down.' He indicated that 'an atheist's disappointment in and resentment of his own father unconsciously justifies his rejection of God'. This last statement is going to return to bite Freud on the proverbial backside, but we will come to that in a moment. The important thing is to understand what Feuerbach and Freud are doing, what their *methodology* is, namely, begin by assuming religious beliefs to be wrong, and indeed harmful, and explain them away in terms of having 'father complexes' and the like. If they are right, then who needs to look at evidence and use reason? Thus, when Freud as a young man did believe in God, according to his own theory, God was just a projection of his Dad 'writ large'.

Dawkins' delusion

More recently Professor Richard Dawkins has adopted a similar line of approach. A few years ago he likened religious belief to a 'mental virus'—a false belief which infects your mind the way a virus infects your body.[3] Look at the symptoms, he says. People don't adopt religion after carefully weighing the evidence; faith is 'caught' very much the way

---

3. Richard Dawkins, 'Viruses of the Mind', Free Inquiry, Summer 1993. Online: http://www.simonyi.ox.ac.uk/dawkins/WorldOfDawkins-archive/Dawkins/Work/Articles/1993-summervirusesofmind.shtml. Accessed 28 August 2006.

a cold is. It spreads from one person to another like an infection, especially in families. For those who convert, says Dawkins, an evangelist may be the infectious agent. To explain this he develops a concept called 'memes'. Memes are ideas or beliefs which are analogous to genes (that is our hereditary material) in that they can replicate and spread rapidly infecting people's minds. And so he writes, 'Examples of memes are tunes, ideas, catchphrases, clothes fashions, ways of making pots or building arches. Just as genes propagate themselves in the gene pool by leaping from body to body via sperm or eggs, so memes propagate themselves in the meme pool by leaping from brain to brain.' (*The Selfish Gene*).[4] In the TV programme which appeared in the UK entitled 'The Root of all Evil', he dismissed all religious faith as, 'an indulgence of irrationality that is nourishing extremism, division and terror.' This is the same approach as Freud and Feuerbach—religion is *assumed* to be a mental aberration, something irrational, and if that is the case you don't take people who hold those views seriously and you certainly don't *reason* with them, instead you find a *cause* for their beliefs, in this case the notion of a meme—and that explains everything.

It reminds me of the story of a man who visited his doctor because he believed himself to be dead. The doctor tried to give him all sorts of reasons why his belief that he was dead was mistaken. But the man insisted, 'No I *am* dead'. Eventually the doctor persuaded him that, 'dead men don't bleed'—especially those who had been dead as long as he

---

4. Richard Dawkins, *The Selfish Gene*, 2nd Edition (Oxford University Press) 1989, p 192

claimed to have been. Rather sneakily the doctor then took out a scalpel and nicked the man's hand. The man looked in horror at the blood oozing from the wound only to exclaim, 'Dead men *do* bleed after all!' What has reason got to do with a person in *that* state? Similarly, what has reason to do with people who believe in a personal God any more than a person who really believes in the tooth fairy? This is the upshot of Dawkin's argument.

Here, then, is the question for the Christian; is belief in God wholly irrational, only to be explained away in terms of father complexes and mental viruses? What would Lewis say? In fact, what *did* he say?

The power of the story—*The Silver Chair*
First of all, let's see how Lewis deals with this approach of debunking belief in terms of wish fulfilment and irrational ideas in the sixth of the seven Narnia books, *The Silver Chair*. This is set in a dark underground world ruled by a witch—the Lady of the Green Kirtle. The Prince who comes from the world of Narnia with its sun and moon and trees and hills tries to persuade her that the dark, dingy world she inhabits is not the only world, but there is a better world—Narnia. And so sceptically, the witch gets the prince to tell her about what he calls 'the sun' of which there is no equivalent in the underworld to which she belongs. In response the prince used an analogy: *the sun is like a lamp*. This is how the story proceeds and consider it very carefully in the light of the objections of people like Freud and Dawkins that the 'Christian World' composed of God, angels, demons, and morality is an illusion: The Prince says to the witch, 'You see that lamp. It is round and yellow and gives light to the whole

room; and hangeth moreover from the roof. Now that thing which we call the sun is like the lamp, only far greater and brighter. It giveth light to the whole Overworld and hangeth in the sky.' The witch comes back to this very quickly with her reply, '"Hangeth from what, my Lord?" asked the witch; and then while they were all still thinking how to answer her, she added with another of her soft, silver laughs. "You see? When you try to think out clearly what this *sun* must be you cannot tell me. You can only tell me it is like the lamp. Your *sun* is a dream; and there is nothing in that dream that was not copied from the lamp. The lamp is the real thing; the *sun* is but a tale, a children's story."'[5]

Substitute the word 'God' for 'sun' and you have pure Freud and Dawkins! They are using the argument of the witch. At first sight the argument seems so sophisticated and 'reasonable', but we know it is completely *unreasonable* for we know there *is* a sun. Here in a children's story C. S. Lewis is showing that when you look at the argument like this, much of the force is taken away.[6]It also does give a sad picture of what Dawkins is proposing, for within his 'worldview' we are only left with a dark underworld, a diminished little 'reality' which is presented as the whole of reality, with the accompanying cry, 'Isn't it wonderful!'

The power of reason—Bulverism
Long before Narnia was conceived in the fertile mind of

---

5. C. S. Lewis, *The Silver Chair* (HarperCollins,2002) pp 401–402

6. 'Lewis has borrowed this from Plato—while using Anselm of Canterbury and Rene Descartes as intermediaries—thus allowing classical wisdom to make an essentially Christian point.' Alister McGrath—*C. S. Lewis—A Life* (Hodder and Stoughton, 2013), p 302

Lewis, he wrote an essay to expose the sheer hopelessness of this way of arguing and gave it the name, 'Bulverism'.[7] Remember how folk like Freud and Dawkins *explain away* beliefs by saying that they are the product of something else which is irrational. Here is Lewis in his essay unpacking the implications,

> The Freudians have discovered that we exist as bundles of complexes ... Nowadays the Freudian will tell you to go and analyze the hundred: you will find that they all think Elizabeth [I] a great queen because they all have a mother-complex. Their thoughts are psychologically tainted at the source ... Now this is obviously great fun; but it has not always been noticed that there is a bill to pay for it. There are two questions that people who say this kind of thing ought to be asked. The first is, are all thoughts thus tainted at the source, or only some? The second is, does the taint invalidate the tainted thought—in the sense of making it untrue—or not? If they say that all thoughts are thus tainted, then, of course, we must remind them that Freudianism and Marxism are as much systems of thought as Christian theology ... The Freudian and Marxian are in the same boat with all the rest of us, and cannot criticize us from outside. They have sawn off the branch they were sitting on. If, on the other hand, they say that the taint need not invalidate their thinking, then neither need it invalidate ours. In which case they have saved their own branch, but also saved ours along with it.

C. S. Lewis is simply arguing that if *all* thoughts are poisoned in some way, then so is the thought that all

---

7. C.S Lewis, 'Bulverism', *First and Second Things* (Fount, 1985), pp 13–18.

thoughts are poisoned so why should we take *that* thought seriously? If Christian thoughts are poisoned and are the result of complexes, why should Freudianism be exempt? If it is exempt, then why not Christianity also? It is an argument that claims far too much and boomerangs back on the claimant! (The philosophical term is that it is 'self-referentially refuting').

Lewis goes on:

You must show that a man is wrong before you start explaining why he is wrong. The modern method is to assume without discussion that he is wrong and then distract his attention from this (the only real issue) by busily explaining how he became so silly. In the course of the last fifteen years I have found this vice so common that I have had to invent a name for it. I call it 'Bulverism'. Some day I am going to write the biography of its imaginary inventor, Ezekiel Bulver, whose destiny was determined at the age of five when he heard his mother say to his father—who had been maintaining that two sides of a triangle were together greater than a third—'Oh you say that because you are a man.' 'At that moment', E. Bulver assures us, 'there flashed across my opening mind the great truth that refutation is no necessary part of argument. Assume that your opponent is wrong, and explain his error, and the world will be at your feet. Attempt to prove that he is wrong or (worse still) try to find out whether he is wrong or right, and the national dynamism of our age will thrust you to the wall.' That is how Bulver became one of the makers of the Twentieth Century.

This is exactly where we are today in the 21st century. Forget argument and reason, assume your opponent is just wrong or stupid or both and explain his ideas away by appealing to pseudoscience. This happened to me a few years ago when I was in Jerusalem at the Global Anglican Future Conference (GAFCON). At the same time as that conference there was a large gay pride event taking place down the road from where we were meeting and I was invited by the BBC to attend and debate with one of its leaders, which I readily did. This then appeared on BBC world news; (you can still watch it on the BBC web site). As you can imagine I received a fair bit of correspondence as a result, not all favourable! One of the most interesting was from someone who was gay who said that my objection to homosexual practice must be because I am repressing a latent homosexuality of my own. This is pure Bulverism. He could not or didn't want to concede that I might have *reasons* to think homosexual practice was wrong and stands as an example of disordered sexuality—so there must be some *psychological* explanation for my position, namely, *I* must be gay but refusing to acknowledge it. Ezekiel Bulver would have been proud![8]

However, as Lewis points out, the argument cuts both ways. In the case of Freud and other atheists, it could be put forward that the reason (cause) why they *do not* believe in God has some basis in *their* childhood, maybe because of some difficulties they had with their fathers, having a psychological explanation and thus having no sufficient intellectual basis at all. This is itself could be construed as a form of wish fulfilment, they *don't wish* there to be a God

---

8. This is a tactic explicitly encouraged by gay activists in the book *After the Ball* by Marshall Kirk and Hunter Madsen (Plume Books, 1989)

and so find arguments to back up their position which has its roots elsewhere.

In his book *Faith of the Fatherless*, Paul Vitz explores Freud's claim mentioned earlier that 'an atheist's disappointment in and resentment of his own father unconsciously justifies *his* rejection of God'.[9] What he did was to examine the childhood of the most famous atheists of all time—Nietzsche, Hume, Russell, Hitler, Stalin, Mao Zedong, Sartre and others and he concluded, 'We find a weak, dead or abusive father in every case'. In many instances the link between atheism and a defective father is openly acknowledged. Don't misunderstand what I am saying, this doesn't mean that atheism is wrong, it just means that you can't settle the validity of a belief (including atheism) on the basis of another, such as psychological predilections, you need to use *reason and evidence*.

The same goes for Dawkins' notion of 'memes'. Am I a Christian because I picked up a religious virus from someone at school? Dawkins would seem to think so. The same could be argued for Dawkins' atheism. Supposing the reason Dawkins is an atheist is because his beliefs were 'caught' from Mr Smedly his atheistic science teacher at school. Does that mean what he believes about the meaninglessness of life and evolutionism as a guiding metanarrative are to be dismissed as mere bouts of having caught the 'atheist bug'? Of course not! Even the idea of a meme could be the result of a meme and so it really is fruitless and futile concept. *How* we learn

---

9. Paul Vitz, *Faith of the Fatherless: The Psychology of Atheism* (Ignatius Press; 2nd edition, 2013)

about religion or come to hold any belief for that matter, is a separate question from whether or not it is *true*. That has to be decided by looking at the evidence.

This is precisely the point C. S. Lewis was making. Technically this approach of assuming a person to be wrong, and explaining his views away in terms of 'You would believe that wouldn't you? Because you are insecure, frightened of novelty, cowardly and so on'—is called an *ad hominem* argument. It literally means you attack *the man* not his ideas. The tactic is that if you show the man or woman to be 'religious' or bigoted' or what other put-down label you may want to apply, then you won't have to bother yourself with their arguments for you have already decided they are not worth listening to in the first place. The problem is that it marks the end of *all* argument and rational persuasion—you are simply left with bullying tactics, scaremongering and plain abuse. This also marks the end of any civilized society.

Interestingly enough, 'Bulverism' is nothing new for there is a clear example of the opponents of Jesus using this method against him. This is found in Luke 11:14ff, 'Jesus was driving out a demon that was mute. When the demon left, the man who had been mute spoke, and the crowd was amazed. But some of them said, "By Beelzebul, the prince of demons, he is driving out demons." Others tested him by asking for a sign from heaven. Jesus knew their thoughts and said to them: "Any kingdom divided against itself will be ruined, and a house divided against itself will fall. If Satan is divided against himself, how can his kingdom stand? I say this because you claim that I drive out demons by Beelzebul. Now if I drive out demons by Beelzebul, by whom do your followers drive them out? So then, they will be your judges. But if I drive out demons by the finger of God, then the kingdom of God has come upon you.'"

The Pharisees when confronted with a miracle performed by Jesus do not take it as evidence that he was someone special, the Messiah; instead they have already made up their minds that his power is demonic (the cause) and this is used to explain the evidence away so it ceases to *be* evidence.

But notice how Jesus (like Lewis many centuries later) counters the vacuous nature of this approach. Jesus employs the *reduction ad absurdum*.

First, he argues, any kingdom divided against itself is ruined. To claim that this is the work of Satan would mean that he is ruining his own kingdom which doesn't make sense (at this stage—v18—the alternative is implied but not explicitly stated—therefore it must be of God since he is in the Satan-destroying business). Then Jesus presses home the point even further, 'If I am doing this through the power of Satan, then by what power are your exorcists doing it?' As if to say, 'Are they in Satan's employ too? If not, why not? How can you distinguish between what I am doing and what they are doing since the results are the same? So you saw off the branch on which you are sitting.' Then Jesus draws out explicitly the implication of his actions, namely, that if it is by God's power (and not Satan's and that has already been ruled out as an absurdity) then the Kingdom of God has come (v19).

These things need to be borne in mind when it comes to assessing Christianity. The issue is not, who *influenced* me to become a Christian, but rather, do I have any *reasons* for believing it to be true whether I like it or not, regardless who or what influenced me? Here again is C. S. Lewis,

> Christianity claims to give an account of facts—to tell you what the real universe is like. Its account of the universe may be true, or it may not, and once the question is really before you, then your natural inquisitiveness must make you want to know the answer. If Christianity is untrue, then no honest man will want to believe it, however helpful it might be; if it is true, every honest man will want to believe it, even if it gives him no help at all.[10]

Conclusion

It is neither a matter of opinion nor a matter of taste. It is not even a matter of *wanting* something to be true because it will be a valuable prop, rather, it is a matter of whether or not Christianity is *true*. The claim being made is that it *is* true, that when you look at life through the spectacles of the Christian faith, things start to become clear and make sense: you see that there is a God who made us and to whom we are accountable and from whose kind face we have turned our backs. You begin to understand that we are so bad that when the Maker does come to our world, which he did 2,000 years ago as the God-man Jesus, we simply murdered him. But God used this death by crucifixion to be the means of ridding us of our moral guilt and making us into his friends. This Jesus, who has been raised from the dead (a resurrection backed by stacks of factual evidence), invites us to lay down our arms and surrender to his loving rule. That is when we discover,

---

10. C. S. Lewis, 'Man or Rabbit?' in *God in the Dock* (Eerdmans, 1970) p 108

as Jesus said, "If you continue in my word, then you are truly disciples of mine; *and you will know the truth, and the truth will make you free.*" (John 8:31–32)

2

Is the Trinity Biblical?

Introduction

The Bible does not teach the Trinity doctrine. Rather, it says
that there is only one true and eternal God. 'Jehovah our God
is one Jehovah' (Deuteronomy 6:4) He is the Creator-eternal,
almighty, without equal. Jesus is not Almighty God. Jesus lived
on earth as a perfect man and died for imperfect mankind. God
kindly accepted the life of Jesus as a ransom, and thus through
him is the salvation of the faithful. This is God's will.

So reads a tract from the Jehovah's Witnesses, entitled *Who
are Jehovah's Witnesses?* It is obvious that if you were to ask
the question of a Jehovah's Witness, 'Is the Trinity Biblical?'
the answer given would be a resounding 'No'!

A similar sentiment was expressed by Thomas Jefferson,
the Third President of the United States, 'When we shall
have done away with the incomprehensible jargon of the
Trinitarian arithmetic that three are one, and one are three;
when we shall have knocked down the artificial scaffolding,

reared to mask from view the very simple structure of Jesus; when, in short, we shall have unlearned everything which has been taught since his day, and got back to the pure and simple doctrines he taught, we shall then be truly and worthily his disciples.'

Let it be said at the outset that there is a sense in which that statement by the Jehovah's Witnesses is correct. Strictly speaking, the Bible does not *teach* the Trinity doctrine in such a way that you can turn to a passage which is the equivalent to the statement of faith from Deuteronomy 6:4 for example, "Hear O Israel: the LORD our God, the LORD is one', such that we might read something along the lines of, 'The LORD your God is one God who in his oneness exists as three persons, Father, Son and Holy Spirit.' No such verse exists. That kind of way of formulating doctrine came later in the early church in the form of certain creeds like the Nicene Creed for example. It would be more accurate to say that the Bible *reflects* and *expresses* the doctrine of the Trinity and does so in a variety of different and surprising ways. If this is the case, as I hope to show, then it follows that both the Jehovah Witnesses and Thomas Jefferson are monumentally wrong. As we shall see, Jesus spoke, and his disciples wrote, in such ways that their teaching *requires* the doctrine of the Trinity, nothing less will do justice to the data of the New Testament. However, it is not just a matter of picking out certain proof texts (although there are passages which cannot be understood in any other way except on the basis that God is three persons in one being), but rather that it is that the Biblical revelation in general and the New Testament in particular proceeds according to the belief that God is Triune. There is the 'une'—unity or oneness of God, and the 'tri'—the

Father, the Son and the Holy Spirit—three distinct persons, but co-equally and co-eternally Yahweh God.

The Biblical portrayal of the one true God, as opposed to false ideas of God—both ancient and modern—is that he is Triune and the whole edifice of the Christian faith rests upon this foundation.

The Trinity—'a given'

What is so striking about Trinitarian belief is that it permeates the whole of the New Testament and is assumed by the first Christians without them feeling the need to give arguments or reasons to back up their stance. This in itself is impressive because most of these Christians were Jews, and the one thing which marked out the Jews from any other race on earth was that they were passionately monotheistic—believing in only *one* God.

One of the earliest Jewish declarations of faith, which has just been referred to is the *Shema* of Deuteronomy 6:4—'Hear O Israel: the LORD our God, the LORD is one.' Not two or three or 26—but one. The word used here, translated 'one' is '*echad*' which allows for some sort of complexity or plurality within that oneness. The same word (*echad*) is used of husband and wife becoming 'one' flesh in Genesis 2:24 through the act of sexual union, or the gathering of the tribes of Israel together as 'one' man in Judges 20:1. So an over-translation of this verse would be: 'Hear O Israel: The Lord our God, the Lord is *oneness*.'[1]

---

1. See Graeme Goldsworthy, *Gospel and Wisdom* (Paternoster, 1995), p161, and also the comment of Gordon Jessup, *No Strange God* (Olive Press, 1976), 'It has been suggested by at least one notable Jewish scholar and professor, that there was

Similarly, the early Christians were passionate about that same belief and would have given no quarter to, for example, the view of the Romans that there were many gods. This was the Roman pantheon. Therefore we find the apostle Paul writing to Christians in pagan Corinth, 'So, then, about eating food sacrificed to idols: We know that an idol is nothing at all in the world and that there is no God but *one*' (pure monotheism). However, in the next breath Paul goes on to say, '*Yet* for us there is but one God, the Father from whom all things came and for whom we live; and there is but one Lord (and remember Lord in the Old Testament is the name of God, Yahweh), Jesus Christ, through whom all things came and through whom we live' (1 Corinthians 8:4-6). Thus we have one God—and yet he is at *least* two persons—the Father and the Son.

Note how Jesus is spoken of in *exactly* the same terms as God the Father, that is, as Creator and Sustainer of the universe. Paul was not stupid, someone who would easily get his arithmetic wrong! Nor was he someone who was starting a new religion, he was a Jew of Jews, a 'One God' man all the way to the death if needs be (Philippians 3:2-6). And yet without having any sense of awkwardness, Paul speaks of Jesus as being equally God with the Father as if it were the

---

a time when Judaism could have accepted a Trinitarian doctrine of God. By the time of Maimonides, Christian anti-Jewish behaviour had made this emotionally impossible. From his time onwards it has also been intellectually impossible (except by the grace of God) for an Orthodox Jew to believe in a God whose Unity is so complex that it can also be called Trinity.' p 105. It was the 12th century Jewish philosopher, Maimonides who introduced the use of the word *yachid*, which is related to *echad* but which emphasises the solitary nature of oneness.

most natural thing in the world. The question is, why? How did it happen? We shall see why and how in a moment.

However, before we do so let me make a few preliminary remarks:

First, belief in the Trinity is a matter of *revelation* and not *speculation*. Contrary to what the Jehovah's Witnesses teach, this was not something dreamt up by speculative theologians in the 4th century; it is something which is part of the very fabric of the revelation we have of God's plan of redemption in the Bible. Most certainly it was the case that later theologians tried to put that belief together in words which would preserve and clearly express the Bible's revelation, but they didn't invent it, rather they expounded it.

Secondly, the whole notion of the Trinity is *unique* because God is unique. It simply isn't possible to point to anything else in creation and say, 'There, the Trinity is like that', because God as Trinity is not like anything or anyone else. While we may sometimes try to use illustrations, like the idea that water can be found in three states—liquid, gas and solid, yet all are composed of water; such illustrations break down when applied to God, because he is not remotely like that at all. That illustration if pressed leads to the heresy called 'modalism' which the early church condemned.[2]

---

2. The first person to use the term 'Trinity' (*trinitas*), with its association of 'Tri-unity', was Tertullian, from Carthage (c AD 160—220). He wrote to counter the heretic Praxeas who taught that the Son had no independent existence and that the Father and the Son were really one and the same being. Praxeas was quite crude in the way he put this. He said that it was God the Father who descended into the Virgin's womb in order to become his own Son and so it was God the

The Trinity is in a class all by itself. It is *sui generis*, which is why it makes it very difficult, but not impossible, for us to get some conceptual grasp of the doctrine, 'In his Trinitarian mode of being, God is unique; and, as there is nothing in the universe like him in this respect, so there is nothing which can help us to comprehend him.'[3] Furthermore, talk of water or shamrocks is to talk about *things*. But things can't love or relate—only persons can do that. This brings us to the heart of who the one true God is—three persons in an ongoing eternal relationship of love which flows out to bring into being and embrace people like you and me. This is something wonderfully expressed by the Puritan divine, Richard Sibbes, 'If God had not a communicative, spreading goodness, he would never have created the world. The Father, Son and Holy Ghost were happy in themselves, and enjoyed one another before the world was. Apart from the fact that God delights to communicate and spread his goodness, there would never had been a creation or redemption.'[4]

This leads on to the third point, that there is always going to be an element of *mystery* due to the limits of our imagination and the greatness of God. The crucial question to be answered is not: 'Can we fully understand it?' But, 'Has God revealed it?' If he has, then we are to believe it because nothing less than a right view of God and so a right view of salvation depends upon it.

Father who died on the cross (this heresy is called *Patripassianism*—in that it was the 'Father' (*pater*) who suffered (*passio*).

3. B. B. Warfield, quoted in Fred G. Zaspel, *The Theology of B. B. Warfield: A Systematic Survey* (Inter Varsity Press, 2010) p.182.

4. Cited by Michael Reeves in *The Good God* (Paternoster, 2012), p. 30.

This is a vitally important point which is brought into focus for us by the great 16th-century Reformer, John Calvin, 'God so proclaims himself the sole God as to offer himself to be contemplated clearly as three persons. Unless we grasp these, only the bare and empty name of God flits about in our brains, to the exclusion of the true God.'[5] To put it bluntly: we must worship and serve the one true and living God, anything else is idolatry. The doctrine of the Trinity teaches us to worship God the Father, God the Son and God the Holy Spirit. The entailment is that if we *don't* do that, then we are not worshipping the true God and so are guilty of the sin of idolatry. All we are left with, in the words of Calvin, is only the 'bare and empty *name* of God' not the reality.

Back to the Bible
How, then, does the Bible reflect the truth about the Trinity?

Let's be Trinitarian in our approach and look at three ways in which it does so.

The Trinity and Christian devotion
First, we see the Trinity in the devotion or worship of the first Christians. We have already observed that the early Christians were dyed in the wool monotheists—'one God only' people. And yet they offer worship to God as Father, God as Son and God as Holy Spirit. There are little phrases which readers of the Bible may take for granted but which are packed with theological dynamite which reflect this.

In the first place we have the *greetings* such as 1 Thessalonians 1:1, 'To the church of the Thessalonians *in*

---

5. John Calvin, *Institutes*, 1:13.2, Ed John T. McNeill (Westminster Press, 1960).

God the Father *and* the Lord Jesus Christ.' We may be able
to see how this group of Christians might have some mystical
union with God, but how can they be 'in' a mere man—Jesus?
Of course they can't if he is a mere man, but they can if he is
God. What Paul is doing is putting the two together—God
the Father and God the Son, as if to say, 'these two who are
God, are one God and so the only God who exists and you
Christians gathering in Thessalonica are *in* him.'

Secondly, there are the *blessings,* for example, 2 Corinthians
13:14, 'May the grace of our Lord Jesus Christ and the love
of God and the fellowship of the Holy Spirit be with you
all.' Again, we are so familiar with these words that their
profound significance and oddity are lost on us. Jews knew
where grace (*charis*) came from—God. They knew where love
(*agape*) came from—God. They also knew where fellowship
(*koinonia*) came from—God. Yet, there was only *one* God,
and he is the source of all three blessings—how? Because
God is Father, Son and Holy Spirit. Notice too, how Jesus
is placed before God the Father in this Trinitarian blessing,
underscoring his equality with the Father, and, we may also
add, the Spirit.

Thirdly, we have the *praises* as we find in Ephesians 1:1–11.
Here Paul traces all the blessings of salvation to the Father,
who chose us; to Christ who redeemed us by his blood; and
to the Holy Spirit who seals our final inheritance. 'Praise
be to the God and Father of our Lord Jesus Christ ... he
(Father) chose us in him before the creation of the world ...
in (Christ) we have redemption through his blood ... having
believed you were marked in him with a seal, the promised
Holy Spirit.' Paul is overflowing with praise—not to some

vague idea of 'God'—a 'mere name', but to a God who is personally known as Father, Son and Holy Spirit.

The next big question is: from where did these first believers get their belief and practice to worship God as Father, Son and Holy Spirit, being mindful that they were Jews, having imbibed with their mother's milk the belief that there is only one God and to worship so called other gods or human beings is idolatry? They certainly didn't form a committee to come up with the idea! The most obvious source for their 'Trinitarian consciousness' is none other than the Lord Jesus Christ himself and his followers' experience of him and his teaching.

The experience of Jesus and Trinity

Let's take the experience of Jesus and consider one episode which pinpoints this—Jesus' baptism. This is what we read in Luke's account, 'When all the people were being baptized, Jesus was baptized too. And as he was praying, heaven was opened and the Holy Spirit descended on him in bodily form like a dove. And a voice came from heaven: "You are my Son, whom I love; with you I am well pleased."' (Luke 3:21–22). Right at the beginning of Jesus' public ministry we have the three persons of the Godhead present. This only makes sense if faith in Christ is also a response to the Father who speaks from heaven and an expectation of the power of the Spirit, represented symbolically as a dove. It follows that we can only know Christ fully if we also know the Father who sent him and we receive the Spirit of truth, sent by Jesus after his ascension back to the Father. As we come to Jesus as God the Son, then we come to know God the Father, believing, because God the Spirit has come into our hearts to enable us to have saving trust.

The teaching of Jesus and Trinity

As far as the teaching of Jesus is concerned there are plenty of places one could turn to (especially John 14–16) but we will just focus on one passage at the end of Matthew's Gospel—chapter 28:19ff. This is often called the 'Great Commission' when the disciples received their marching orders from Jesus. He says that followers (disciples) are to be made from all nations and baptized into '*the* name (singular) of the Father and of the Son and of the Holy Spirit'. The wording is very precise and highly significant. Jesus *doesn't* say into the '*names* of the Father, the Son and the Holy Spirit' (plural), because that would mean there are three gods. The god called 'father', the god called 'son' and the god called 'Holy Spirit.'— tritheism. Neither does he say, in the name of the Father, Son and Holy Spirit' ' without 'Son' and 'Spirit' having the definite article placed before them, for that formulation would give us only one God appearing in three different *guises*—sometimes he appears as Son, sometimes he reveals himself in the form of Father and at other times as Spirit. This is modalism.

We need to consider this very carefully: it is *the name* (and remember, 'the name' for the Jew meant the name 'Yahweh', a name a pious Jew would not even utter)—emphasizing that there is only *one* God. Nonetheless, this is the one God who is *the* Father, *the* Son and *the* Holy Spirit, and so each member of the Godhead maintains their distinctiveness. They share the one name—Yahweh—LORD, the 'godness' if you will, whilst remaining three distinct identities, the Father, the Son and the Holy Spirit. That is what the Trinity is. Jesus implicitly taught it; the early Christians assumed and believed it; and we are to do the same.

This makes it clear that the early Christians symbolized the belief that salvation was *entirely* from God by people being baptized into the name of the Trinity, which brings us to the second area which reflects the Trinity.

The Trinity and salvation

It was the experience and revelation of God's rescue plan itself—the Gospel—which *demanded* belief in the Trinity.

Three passages from the Bible underscore this:

2 Corinthians 5:19–21, '*God* was in Christ reconciling the world to himself, not counting men's sins against them.' The one involved was not just part of God, or a mere man who co-operated with God—but *God* in Christ.

John 3:16, '*God* so loved the world that he gave his one and only *Son* so that whoever believes in him will not perish but have eternal life.' If salvation is *entirely* the work of *God,* then the Son who is sent must be God too. Otherwise it is God *plus* 'another'.

Hebrews 9:13–14 shows us the role of the Spirit in what is often called 'the economy of salvation'. Contrasting Jesus' sacrificial death on the cross with the Old Testament sacrificial system we read: 'The blood of goats and bulls and the ashes of a heifer sprinkled on those who are ceremonially unclean sanctify them so that they are outwardly clean. How much more, then, will the blood of Christ, who through the eternal *Spirit* offered himself unblemished to God, cleanse our consciences from acts that lead to death, so that we may serve the living God!' The writer is saying that Jesus who was both priest and victim on the altar of the cross, offered himself as a sacrifice for our sins in the power of the Holy Spirit. We also know the Holy Spirit to be God because Paul spells that out for us in 2 Corinthians 3:17: 'Now the *Lord is* the Spirit, and where the Spirit of the Lord is there is freedom.' In other words, the whole of the Godhead is actively involved in saving us. That our salvation has a threefold source is also taught by the apostle Peter—'To God's chosen people—chosen according to the foreknowledge of *God the Father*, through the sanctifying work of *the Spirit*, for obedience to *Jesus Christ*, sprinkled with his blood—1 Peter 1:2. The Christian's praise is meant to be fuelled by the thought that so great is God's love and so great is our need that *all* the persons of the Trinity are involved in our rescue. The Father decreed it, the Son executed it and the Spirit applies it and so God's Triune love guarantees it!

What is at stake?

Let's think about what is at stake negatively if the Jehovah's Witnesses and Thomas Jefferson are right that God is not triune.

If there is no Trinity, then Jesus who died on the cross is not *God* dying in our place, but a human being who dies to save us *from* God. If this is so, then we are not saved *by* God, but saved *from* God and so God is not our Saviour, but a man (although it is difficult to see how a mere man could save us).

If there is no Trinity, then the work of salvation cannot be the work of God, because for it to be entirely of God it requires *God* to be the priest who *offers* himself as the sacrifice; it requires *God* to be the one who *receives* the sacrifice and it must be *God* who *applies* the work of that sacrifice to our lives. In other words, you need God the Son who died on the cross to redeem us, God the Father who accepts the sacrifice and forgives us, and God the Holy Spirit to work within us. In short, you need the Trinity in order to be saved.

This was the experience of the first Christians when they embraced the Gospel.

The 19th-century theologian B. B. Warfield describes what people find when they become Christians, in the following way, 'By means of this doctrine (the Christian believer) is able to think clearly and consequently of his threefold relation to the saving God, experiencing him as Fatherly love sending a redeemer, as redeeming love executing redemption, as saving love applying redemption; all manifestations in distinct methods and by distinct agencies of the one seeking and saving love of God.'[6]

The Trinity and communion

Thirdly, we need the Trinity if we are going to experience communion, or fellowship (*koinonia*) with God and with each other.

How is the believer brought into a personal, spiritual relationship with God and so with each other as the Body of Christ? The answer is: by the Trinity.

Paul writes in 1 Corinthians 12:4–6: 'There are different kinds of gifts, but the same *Spirit*. There are different kinds of

---

6. Cited in Fred G. Zaspel, *The Theology of B. B. Warfield: A Systematic Survey* (Inter Varsity Press, 2010), p 190.

service, but the same *Lord* (Jesus). There are different kinds of working, but the same God (Father) works all of them in all men.' There is *one* God but there are *three* persons within the Godhead, each person having a different function to perform within the overall economy of our salvation. The term 'gifts' (*charismata*) tells us *what* God *the Spirit* gives—they are love gifts. The term 'service' (*diakonia*) ministries—tells us what *the Son* gives them *for*—service for others. The term workings or energizings (*energemata*), tells us *how* God *the Father* brings them into operation in our lives—by his power. These gifts to the church which come from God the Holy Spirit are meant to enable us to express the servanthood of the Son by the enabling power of the God the Father. In other words, you would not have the *church* if there were no Trinity!

To summarise what is at stake with this belief: no Trinity=no salvation; no Trinity=no church; no Trinity=no Christianity.

But we *do* have the Trinity: there is one God who exists within the eternity of his own glorious being as Father, Son and Holy Spirit. Indeed, you cannot have a truly *Christian* experience without the Trinity. To be sure, people believe in a so called 'god', but that is all it will remain—an idea, cold and distant, mainly something cerebral or, as Calvin put it, 'a name flitting around one's brain' like a pinball. Dr Michael Reeves underscores this point by drawing attention to the fact that it is belief in the Trinity which marks out Christianity from all the world religions:

> … what makes Christianity absolutely distinct is the identity of our God. Which God we worship: that is the article of faith that stands before all others. The bedrock of our faith

is nothing less than God himself, and every aspect of the Gospel—creation, revelation, salvation—is only Christian in so far as it is the creation, revelation and salvation of this God, the triune God. I could believe in the death of a man called Jesus. I could believe in his bodily resurrection, I could even believe in a salvation by grace alone; but if I do not believe in this God, then, quite simply, I am not a Christian. And so, because the Christian God is triune, the Trinity is the governing centre of all Christian belief, the truth that shapes and beautifies all others. The Trinity is the cockpit of all Christian thinking.[7]

Similarly Dr David Broughton Knox writes:

> The doctrine of the Trinity is the foundation of the Christian religion. Unless this doctrine is held firmly and truly, it is not possible to be a Christian. For the Christian is one who acknowledges Jesus as Lord, yet adheres to the religion of the Bible which emphasises so strongly that there is only one God.[8]

The Trinity is vital for authentic Christianity.

This is the way Dr Peter Adam describes authentic Christian experience:

> Life caught up in God is more like relating to a loving community than it is like relating to a loving individual. We turn to the Father; and he gives up the Son and the Spirit; we turn to the Son, and he shows us the Father and breathes the

---

7. Michael Reeves, *The Good God* (Paternoster, 2012), pp. xiii–xiv.
8. D. Broughton Knox, 'God in Trinity' in *Selected Works, Volume I, The Doctrine of God*, ed. Tony Payne (Matthias Media, 2001), p 73.

Spirit upon us; we turn to the Spirit, and he shows us the Father
and the Son.[9]

The Three-Personal God

Are there any illustrations we can use to help us understand
the Trinity? Not really, because as we have already seen, God
is absolutely unique. However, there is one illustration which,
while not 'explaining' the Trinity as such, does help us to be
content with the limitations of our knowledge.

The illustration comes from C. S. Lewis in his book *Mere
Christianity*[10] in which he argues as follows:

In space we can move three ways—left or right, backwards
or forwards, up or down. These are the three dimensions. If
we were using only one dimension, we would only be able
to draw a straight line. With two dimensions we can draw a
figure—maybe a square. But with three dimensions you can
build that up into a solid body—a cube like a lump of sugar.
The point is you advance to more real and complicated levels,
but not leaving the lower levels behind, rather they are taken
up *into* the higher levels. He says that it is a little like that
when we think of God as Triune. The human level is if you
like at the simple and empty level. On the human level one
person is one being, any two persons are separate beings, just
as in two dimensions, on a piece of paper, one square is one
figure and two squares—two figures. But on the Divine level,
it is like a third dimension, you still find the personalities but

---

9. Dr Peter Adam, *The Trinity—What Difference Does it Make?* (Unpublished
paper, Ridley College, Melbourne, 2004).

10. C. S. Lewis, 'The Three-Personal God' in *Mere Christianity* (Fount, 1978),
pp. 137–141.

they are combined in new ways which we on our simple level can't imagine. In God's dimension, you find this wonderful being who is three persons while remaining one being, just as a cube is six squares while remaining one cube.

As with any illustration this has its limitations. The main problem with it is that it is a static picture of *dimensions*, whereas God as he has revealed himself to us in Scripture is a dynamic of interrelated *persons*. Of course Lewis is fully aware of this which is why he entitled his chapter, 'The Three-Personal God'. What this illustration does help to serve, however, is that there is no inherent contradiction in the idea of God as Trinity any more than there is an inherent contradiction between squares and cubes.

Conclusion

The doctrine of the Trinity arises out of the teaching of the Bible itself and in turn shapes our reading of the Bible. It is decisive for authentic *Christian* experience. As Michael Reeves concludes, 'The irony could not be thicker: what we assume would be a dull or peculiar irrelevance turns out to be the source of all that is good in Christianity. Neither a problem or a technicality, the triune being of God is the vital oxygen of Christian life and joy.'[11]

11. Michael Reeves, *The Good God* (Paternoster, 2012) p. xvi.

3

Is God Female?

Introduction

The Franciscan Sisters Cecilia Corcoran and Linda Mershon created a program entitled, *'Retrieving the Feminine Soul Through Ancient Myth and Image.'* This is an invitation to women and men who are searching for the female Divine and seeking wholeness and holiness. It is an exploration of ancient, indigenous feminine images of the Divine in an attempt to bring back traditional richness to our Christian traditions—so it is claimed. The program looks at past stories and asks *what do they mean, what do they tell us today?* Audrey Murray, a parishioner of the church of St Joan of Arc and participant in these experiential travel seminars, explains the impact the programs have had on her life. 'The trips were a life changing experience,' she says. 'I hear about the feminine God at St. Joan and I know that God is more than Father. I was able to move the idea of God as feminine from my head to my heart and experience the feminine God for the first time in my life.' So for her it was a good thing—she feels closer to God through it. Who would want to argue with that?

Christa and the Bakerwoman God

Some have gone so far as to suggest that *Christ* should be thought of as feminine. Back in 1993 a service took place at Manchester Cathedral called *'Coming out of the Shadows— Women overcoming Violence'* in which a female figure on a crucifix referred to as 'Christa', was paraded down the aisle. The publisher, LBI Institute, released a Bible entitled: *Judith Christ of Nazareth, The Gospels of the Bible, Corrected to Reflect that Christ Was a Woman, Extracted from Matthew, Mark, Luke and John.* This new 'Bible' includes: The Parable of the Prodigal Daughter and The Lady's Prayer together with other revised favourite passage, such as Luke 2:4, which reads, 'And Joseph went to Bethlehem to be enrolled with Mary, his wife, who was then pregnant. And she brought forth her firstborn child. And her name was chosen to be Judith.'

At a more modest level some would argue that there is a feminine side to the divine and that this should be reflected in our creeds and prayers. Thus we have these two samples from a World Council of Churches conference held in the early 1990s.

First, a creed:

I believe in God, MOTHER-FATHER-SPIRIT who called the world into being, who created men and women and set them free to live in love, in obedience and community.

I believe in God, who because of love for HER creation, entered the world to share our humanity, to rejoice and to despair, to set before us the paths of life and death; to be rejected, to die, but finally to conquer death and to bind the world to HERSELF.

Secondly, a prayer:

> Bakerwoman God, I am your living bread. Strong, brown, Bakerwoman God. I am your low, soft and being-shaped loaf. I am your rising bread, well-kneaded by some divine and knotty pair of knuckles, by your warm earth-hands. I am bread well-kneaded. Put me in your fire, Bakerwoman God, put me in your own bright fire. Break me, Bakerwoman God. I am broken under your caring Word. Drop me in your special juice in pieces. Drop me in your blood.

The 'Transformations Steering Group' of the Church of England issued a public call to the bishops to encourage more 'expansive language and imagery about God'.[1] Hilary Cotton, chair of Women and The Church (WATCH), has said 'The reality is that in many churches up and down the country something more than the almost default male language about God is already being used.' She further claims, 'it is entirely appropriate to express our worship toward God as a female presence,' and 'that having women bishops makes it particularly obvious that ... to continue to refer to God purely as male is just unhelpful to many people now.'

It is obvious that the question: 'Is God female?' is not at all a frivolous one, it is serious.

---

1. John Bingham, the *Daily Telegraph*, May 3rd, 2015.

Right thinking

We have to be careful not to draw wrong inferences from our thinking. For example, if we conclude that God is not female, does it mean that we are right to say God is 'male'? Given that in John 4:24 Jesus tells the Samaritan woman that God is 'spirit', this might lead some to conclude that he is neither. Does this then mean it would be better to refer to God as an 'it', as many tend to think of the Holy Spirit anyway?

If we try and define what we understand as male or female in terms of chromosome component, sex organs and the like, then it is patently absurd to think of God as female or male.[2] However, when we turn to the Bible there is no doubt that the masculine pronoun is used of God exclusively. God is referred to as 'He', 'Him' 'His'. God is *never* spoken of as 'She', 'Her' or 'Hers'. In some ways this is may seem odd given that the nations which surrounded Israel did have female gods, and also given the fact that the Bible does ascribe feminine attributes to God, like compassionate nursing

---

2. '... the use of male pronouns for God does not mean that God is male, except when these pronouns are used to refer to the male humanity of the incarnate Christ. In terms of his divine nature God is neither male nor female, but transcends both. When we say that a human being is male we mean that he has certain physical and psychological characteristics that distinguish him from a human female. As a purely spiritual being without a female counterpart with different sexual characteristics the God described in the Bible cannot be male in this sense and neither can he be female. In the words of Stephen Sapp 'the distinction between the sexes is a creation by God since there is no such distinction on the divine level; the polarity of the sexes belongs to the created order and not to God.' Martin Davie, 'On the Use of Pronouns'—http://anglicanmainstream.org/on-the-use-of-pronouns/

(Isaiah 49:15), motherly comfort (Isaiah 66:13) and carrying an infant (Isaiah 46:3).[3]

But then again, non-personal imagery is also used of God, such that he is described as our 'rock'. Does it then follow that we are to conceive of God in terms of mineral composition and solidity? If not, why not?

Mind your language

What we are being introduced to here is what is appropriate and inappropriate language by which we are to speak about God who, by definition, is beyond our full comprehension. So, if God is to be thought of as 'Father', then he is both like *and* unlike any earthly Father we have ever known.

Instinctively we may react for or against these ideas. Some feel attracted to the notion of a feminine side to the divine, other are pretty blunt in denouncing it as heresy. But there are two basic questions which need to be answered regardless of matters of personal preference, namely, what is true and how can we know?

Let's think about these in reverse order.

How can we know?

Here is *the* question: How can we know *anything* about God?

---

3. 'Allowing that one should read the biblical texts in historical context, it turns out that once we understand those contexts properly, the Bible is actually remarkably *male-orientated* in its talk of God. The Old Testament world was a world full of goddesses, and there was indeed an abundance of conceptual resources at hand for describing God in feminine terms, or indeed for taking God as female—as Goddess.' Richard S. Briggs, 'Gender and God-talk: Can We Call God 'Mother'? *Themelios* Vol 29, Issue 2, 2004, pp. 18–19.

The fundamental problem we have is that we are finite and God is infinite and so a great chasm is fixed between us; Isaiah 55, 'As the heavens are higher than the earth, so are my ways higher than your ways and my thoughts than your thoughts, says the LORD'. What is more, given the fact that our minds are polluted by sin so our perception of spiritual things is warped, we might be led to conclude that the whole enterprise of knowing God is doomed to failure from the outset. And of course, that would be so, *if* God had not undertaken to cross that chasm and make contact with us.

How is the infinite to communicate to the finite? The answer: by revelation. The Bible tells us that God has done this in two ways. First, by what is called 'natural' or 'general' revelation, that is through the things made and the sense deep down within us that there is a God to whom we are accountable. This is how Paul describes it in Romans 1:19, 'For what can be known about God is plain to them, because God has shown it to them. Ever since the creation of the world his eternal power and divine nature, invisible though they are, have been understood and seen through the things he has made.' But that kind of general revelation doesn't get us very far in knowing what God is like, it just leaves us without excuse for atheism. For a problem comes with what we go on to *do* with that revelation, which is to twist it in our sinfulness, 'So' Paul goes on, 'they are without excuse; for though they knew God, they did not honour him as God or give thanks to him, but they became futile in their thinking, and their senseless minds were darkened. Claiming to be wise, they became fools; and they exchanged the glory of the immortal God for images resembling a mortal human being or birds or four-footed animals or reptiles.' This 'knowledge' may call out to us that there is a God and that he is rational, transcendent and creative. It may also stir within us a sense that we are in some way accountable to him in conjunction with having an inner sense of the divine—what theologian John Calvin called the *sensus divinitatis.* But it doesn't get us very far with regards to knowing God and finding out what this God requires from us. We need something more if we are going to know God truly.

This is where secondly; *special* revelation comes in; *God* communicating to us clearly in terms we can understand. This God has done through the Bible and supremely through the one who is the main character in the Biblical drama, the Lord Jesus Christ.

Sometimes people will object by saying something such as, 'I don't worship the Bible, the written word, I worship Jesus the living word. I want to know a person not a proposition. I don't want an exposition, I want an experience'. However, all of these are false options. How can you know Jesus other than by learning about him from Scripture? The Jesus of faith *is* the Jesus of history and we have no other access to him but by the Bible. Also, isn't it the case that the words of a person reflect what the person is like? If someone makes promises and keeps them then we know they are a reliable person. If they issue warnings and consequences, we know they are a moral person. If they offer words of comfort and love we know them to be a caring person. That seems to be to be a fair summary of the God of the Bible!

We must also remember that words aren't just about information, they are about action. This is vitally important. If I say to my wife, 'I love you'. I am not just imparting some interesting titbit of information about the state of my glands, I am actually *fostering* love, *showing* care, *building* her up, *strengthening* our relationship—*through* words. Not *only* words of course, but words are a vital part of the process. In short, words are fundamental to *covenant* relationships. That is what God does through the Bible which is why Christians refer to it as: 'The Word of God.' This is where we hear God's voice clearly, discover his will, learn his ways, and get to know his person as well as receive his comfort. This is how we can have a covenantal relationship with him.

Get the picture?

However, we need to ask: what is the *nature* of this language God uses to communicate to us in the Bible? To some extent almost all language about God is 'picture language'— metaphorical, what else could it be? Traditionally both Jews and Christians have taken such revelation language to be *analogical.* Metaphors are used which convey some truth or other about the nature and character of God; the trick is deciding which elements are applicable and which aren't.[4]

For example, take the 23rd Psalm and the claim of David

---

4. 'The claim is that all these masculine images for God in the biblical text are working metaphorically, of necessity, since to talk of God is to try to put God into a context where we consider the divine nature from some suggested angle and to see where the image leads us: thus 'God is my rock' or 'shepherd' are two different ways of saying God is like A or B.' Richard. S. Briggs, op cit., p 21. Similarly Dr Martin Davie, writes, 'The reason that nearly all the language we use about God is analogical in this way is because our language is designed to describe our experience of the created order and, with the one exception of the human nature of God the Son, God is not a creature. It follows that we either have to use language analogically when we refer to God or say nothing at all.' 'On the Use of Pronouns'—http://anglicanmainstream.org/on-the-use-of-pronouns/

that, 'The Lord is my shepherd'. How are we to understand that?

There is the literal level of course, where a shepherd goes ahead of his flock with a crook, feeds his sheep with grass and protects them from wolves and bears with his staff. Is that what God is doing? Certainly not literally.

Then there is the analogical level, so we understand God to be *like* or *analogous* to a shepherd in caring, saving, protecting, leading his people and so on. We know that these are the 'points of comparison' because we can turn to other parts of the Bible which depicts God in similar ways.

What is important to grasp is that such images are *God-*given (divine revelation) and not *man* made (human construction). If it were a matter of us simply deciding what we would like to think God as being, then it would be open ended. For instance, the argument, 'I find it helpful as a woman to think of God as feminine for it affirms my gender' could similarly be used by the animal rights activist who says 'I like to think of God as a rat for it affirms my belief in the sanctity of all animal life.' It would then become a theological 'free for all': God is whatever you would like to think 'him' or 'her' or 'it' to be. But if God has given us the pictures and words by which we are to think of him aright, then there are limits set by God himself.

Degrees of correspondence.

The next thing we need to recognize is that different metaphors have different degrees of correspondence. Some correspondence is low and distant, others are high and close. Think of it like a horizontal line with a range of

correspondence between a picture depicting God. At one end
there is just a vague similarity between the image used and
God and at the top end a very close similarity:

Low ─────────────────────────────────────►High

Where along the line would you place the following biblical
images:

Rock; Bridegroom; eagle; King; fortress; shepherd; Father
—all used to depict God?

Would the arrangement not look something like this?

Rock Fortress Eagle Shepherd Bridegroom King Father

Low ─────────────────────────────────────►High

The move is from the less personal to the more personal
with a greater degree of theological development and
co-ordination occurring the further along the line you go.[5]

The Bible, however, does not see the higher correspondence
of revelation, God as Father, as being some arbitrary image
which could be taken and applied to God if it helps us or
discarded if it doesn't. Rather, it seems to indicate that this
is what God is like *in himself* so that *our* ideas of fatherhood

---

5. 'All points of comparison belong to one of four classes: perceptual,
synaesthetic, affective and pragmatic', G.B. Caird, *Language, Imagery and the Bible*
(Duckworth, 1980), p. 145 Perceptual comparisons appeal to the five senses (e.g.
1 Samuel 17:7). Synaesthesia is the use in one connection with one of the senses
which are proper to another, e.g. 'sharp words'. Affective comparisons are those
in which we feel or value, the effect or impression of one thing is compared to
another, e.g. the hearts of Joshua's troops turning to water (Joshua 7:5). Pragmatic
comparison compares the activity or result of one thing with that of another e.g.
love is more heady than wine (Song of Solomon 1:2).

ultimately derive from God who is *the* perfect Father—e.g. Ephesians 3:14-15, 'For this reason I kneel before the Father, from whom all fatherhood in heaven and earth derives its name.'[6] From a pastoral point of view this is of tremendous help to those who, because of their experience of abusive fathers, feel they cannot address God in this way. The fact that they feel abused indicates that there is some standard of *good* fatherhood from which their own fathers have tragically fallen short. The Christian would argue that it is God himself. As we look at what he has said and done in the Bible we then discover why the term Father fits perfectly, he is the supreme model of fatherhood who cares passionately about his children.[7]

When we move on to consider God's eternal being, we discover that the Biblical revelation introduces us to the

---

6. Theologians traditionally distinguish between the *order of being* and the *order of knowing*. This is the difference between how we come to understand God as Father and how his Fatherhood stands as revealed truth which makes human fatherhood both meaningful and possible. The way we may conceive God as father in our thinking may work its way 'up' from our knowledge of human fatherhood, but the reality is grounded the other way around, it derives from God. Thus Athanasius (c.AD 300–373), 'God as father of the Son is the only true Father, and all created paternity is a shadow of the true.' Athanasius, *contra Arian*, 1.23, 24.

7. 'The fact that some people, perhaps even a great many people, have problematic relationships with their human fathers does not by itself invalidate the biblical imagery. God is not to be regarded as a heavenly projection of our earthly fathers and judged accordingly. On the contrary, if there is any connection at all between these two things, it must surely be that God our heavenly father speaks to our human deficiencies in this respect, as in others, and supplies what is missing in them. Beaten and abandoned by an earthly parent we may be, but if that happens we can be sure that God will enfold us in his everlasting arms and comfort us in ways no human being can match.' Gerald Bray, *Yours is the Kingdom. A Systematic theology of the Lord's Prayer* (Inter Varsity Press, 2007, p. 24.

one God who *is* God the Father, eternally related to God the Son by God the Holy Spirit. God is not Father, Mother and Son, or, as in the WCC creed, Father, Mother and Spirit, but Father, Son and Spirit. The person of God the Father is Father by virtue of the fact that he has an eternal Son. The Son is Son by virtue of the fact that he has an eternal Father. Substitute these persons for some other—like daughter or mother and you end up with a different god altogether. The Triune God is *given* to us in the Bible and we have to reckon with it, not abandon it because we may or may not like it or find some other idea preferable.[8]

This is the way C. S. Lewis lays out what is at stake if we abandon biblical imagery in an essay which appears in the book, *God in the Dock,* 'Goddesses have, of course, been worshipped: many religions have had priestesses. But they are religions quite different in character from Christianity ... Since God is in fact not a biological being and has no sex, what can it matter whether we say He or She, Father or Mother, Son or Daughter? Christians think that God Himself has taught us how to speak of Him. To say that it does not matter is to say either that all the masculine imagery is not inspired, is merely human in origin, or else that, though inspired, it is quite arbitrary and unessential. And this is surely intolerable.'[9]

---

8. Thus Tertullian circa AD 200 wrote: 'Whereas other analogical terms like Lord and Judge indicate a merely functional relation to the world, the names Father and Son point to an ontological relationship within the godhead itself.' Tertullian, *adversus Praxean,* 9–10, quoted by Donald G. Bloesch, *A Theology of Word and Spirit: Authority and Method in Theology* (Paternoster, 1992), p 295

9. C. S. Lewis, 'Priestesses in the Church?' in *'God in the Dock'* (Fount, 1970), p. 237

Sometimes it is pointed out that feminine imagery is used in the Bible to describe God. What do we do say to that?

The first thing to say is that it is true that some action or attribute of God is well captured by certain 'feminine' imagery—e.g. Luke 13:34, where Jesus lamenting over Jerusalem and its pending destruction because of its rejection of him says, 'Jerusalem, Jerusalem, the city that kills the prophets and stones those who are sent to it! How often have I desired to gather your children together as a hen gathers her brood under her wings, and you were not willing!' But what you have to ask yourself is this: what aspect of God is that imagery intended to depict? It is not the 'feminine' *per se*, but the protective and sacrificial action of a hen. God is like that in that he is sacrificially protective. However, the imagery of father seems much more integral to God's character and being. He acts like a Father because fatherliness is what he *is* as testified to by his eternal relationship to the Son in a way that 'henness' or 'femaleness' is not.

Neither can we dismiss the revelation of God as a man in the incarnation as if it were incidental. It was as *Jesus* of Nazareth, not *Judith* of Nazareth that the eternal WORD, the Son—came and remains. The fact is a *man* reigns at the centre of the universe thus fulfilling Psalm 8, not simply a 'human being'. Jesus Christ is not sexless, he is male.

Here we have a good example of how Christian doctrines are all linked to each other in some way such that to tamper with one (especially a central doctrine such as the identity of God) has a knock on, deleterious effects on others: 'If God has revealed himself as a Mother-Daughter combination, how would the incarnation of the Daughter have been possible?

She could not have entered the womb of the Virgin Mary, since then not only would she have had two mothers—one divine, and another human—but there would have been no room for the male principal at all … The incarnation of a male avoids unnecessary reduplication of having two mothers and permits both sexes to play a part in the coming of the Saviour.'[10]

Furthermore, each biblical picture of God is carefully co-ordinated with every other image of God. And so one of the most glorious images the Bible gives of God's relationship to his church is that of groom and bride. That image is completely smashed if God is primarily conceived as feminine—except of course, it gives further grist for the mill of the proponents of same-sex marriage. To tamper with the Biblical images of God, even so slightly, results in distorted thinking, corrupt worship and eventually questionable behaviour. I say that because what goes out of the window when God is primarily thought of in feminine terms is holiness and wrath—they simply evaporate.

What is true?

The more fundamental question of course is what is true? If God is the source of all truth and is incapable of lying to us or misleading us, then we have to accept how *he* describes himself as also being true. We therefore happily submit to God's self-revelation because it is a window into how God really is and as such is liberating because we are not left to our own devices groping around in the dark for some image of

10. Gerald Bray, 'Yours is the Kingdom. A Systematic theology of the Lord's Prayer' (Inter Varsity Press, 2007), p 23.

God which might or might not be right—he has told us what
is right.

Let's think for a moment about why God in his revelation in
the Bible is described exclusively by the masculine pronoun—
'He'.

One of the main reasons is that it is a term which preserves
something which is vital to his nature and being, namely,
his transcendence. He is a God who is wholly 'beyond' this
world—a world which is dependent upon him and not the
other way around.

Similarly, when it comes to saving grace. We have to be
born 'from above' said Jesus to Nicodemus (John 3:3), God
by His Spirit gives us this new birth from outside ourselves,
we don't co-operate with him to bring it about. So just as a
universe can't birth itself, a person can't give new birth to
himself or herself—and the masculine imagery preserves
both these truths. In this way the religion of the Bible is vastly
different from pagan religions with their talk of gods and
goddesses bringing things into being—like the Baal religion
of the Canaanites or the Babylonian religion of Marduk and
Tiamat.

Feminine and the valuing of the female
Very briefly let me deal with one argument often made in
favour of re-envisioning God in feminine categories.

It is often said that realizing the feminine in the divine is
of value to women, enhancing their status, in contrast to the
patriarchal nature of the Bible. In reply it has to be said that
this is not simply providing a corrective to Christianity; it

is creating a new religion. To be more precise it is reviving old pagan religions in Christian guise. However, when you carefully look at these religions, women are not particularly valued. In the pagan religions mention in the Bible, the senior god is always male and the female god is given a secondary role. They are linked with fertility which is ironic given the resistance to the idea that woman are seen as mere 'baby factories.' We should not therefore be surprised that such female worship led to temple prostitution, with the women being the losers and men being the oppressive winners.

At a pragmatic level, moves to view God in feminine categories will simply increase the already rapid exit of men from the church. Over the last 30 years there has been an increased feminization of the church, no least in terms of its leadership, which, to be frank is a switch-off for many men. The glory of the revelation of God in Jesus Christ is that he commanded the allegiance of *both* sexes—hardy fishermen like Peter and Andrew and domestic carers like Martha and Mary.

Richard Sibbes, who was a Puritan and a contemporary of Shakespeare, said that our view of God shapes us deeply such that we become what we worship. The God who is Trinity, who exists in an eternal relationship of holy love between Father, Son and Holy Spirit, is the God Christians worship as there is no other. It was to this end that Jesus prayed these words, 'Righteous *Father,* though the world does not *know* you, I know you, and they know that you sent me. I have made you (God as Father) known to them, and will continue to make you known in order that the love you have for me (paternal love) may be in them and that I myself may be in them.' (John 17:25–26). Jesus died that we might know God in this way, so we can call him Father; the Spirit comes into our life so that we can know God this way and cry '*Abba* Father'.

All contrary claims are simply false.

4

If God is so good, why are things so bad?

Introduction

Let me introduce this touchy topic with a story.[1]

Once there was an old man who lived in a tiny village. Although poor, he was envied by all, for he owned a beautiful white horse. Even the king coveted his treasure. A horse like this had never been seen before—such was its splendour, its majesty, its strength. People offered fabulous prices for the steed, but the old man always refused. 'This horse is not a horse to me,' he would tell them. 'It is a person. How could you sell a person? He is a friend, not a possession. How could you sell a friend?' The man was poor and the temptation was great. But he never sold the horse. One morning he found that the horse was not in the stable. The entire village came to see him.

---

1. This parable is an old Chinese story known as the story of 'Sai weng ma' but is told by Max Lucado, 'The Woodcutter's Wisdom', *In the Eye of the Storm* (Word, 1991), pp 144–147

'You old fool,' they scoffed, 'we told you that someone would steal your horse. We warned you that you would be robbed. You are so poor. How could you ever hope to protect such a valuable animal? It would have been better to have sold him. You could have asked whatever price you wanted. Now the horse is gone, and you've been cursed with misfortune.' The old man responded, 'Don't speak too quickly. Say only that the horse is not in the stable. That is all we know; the rest is judgement. If I've been cursed or not, how can you know? How can you judge?' The people contested, 'Don't make us out to be fools! We may not be philosophers, but great philosophy is not needed. The simple fact that your horse is gone is a curse.' The old man spoke again. 'All I know is that the stable is empty, and the horse is gone. The rest I don't know. Whether it is a curse or a blessing, I can't say. All we can see is a fragment. Who can say what will come next?' The people of the village laughed. They thought that the man was mad. They had always thought he was fool; if he wasn't, he would have sold the horse and lived off the money. But instead, he was a poor woodcutter, an old man still cutting firewood and dragging it out of the forest and selling it. He lived hand to mouth in the misery of poverty. Now he had proven that he was, indeed, a fool.

After fifteen days, the horse returned. He hadn't been stolen; he had run away into the forest. Not only had he returned but he had brought a dozen wild horses with him. Once again the village people gathered around the woodcutter and spoke. 'Old man, you were right and we were wrong. What we thought was a curse was a blessing. Please forgive us.' The man responded, 'Once again, you go too far. Say only that the horse is back. State only that a dozen horses returned with him, but don't judge. How do you know if this is a blessing or not? You see only a fragment. Unless you know the whole story, how can you judge? You read only one page of a book. Can you judge the whole book? You read only one word of a phrase. Can you understand the entire phrase? Life is so vast, yet you judge all of life with one page or one word. All you have is a fragment! Don't say that this is a blessing. No one knows. I am content with what I know. I am not perturbed by what I don't.'

'Maybe the old man is right,' they said to one another. So they said little. But down deep, they knew he was wrong. They knew it was a blessing. Twelve wild horses had returned with one horse. With a little bit of work, the animals could be broken and trained and sold for much money. The old man had a son, an only son. The young man began to break the wild horses. After a few days, he fell from one of the horses and broke both legs. Once again the villagers gathered around the old man and cast their judgements. 'You were right,' they said. 'You proved you were right. The dozen horses were not a blessing. They were a curse. Your only son has broken his legs, and now in your old age you have no one to help you. Now you are poorer than ever.'

The old man spoke again. 'You people are obsessed with judging. Don't go so far. Say only that my son broke his legs. Who knows if it is a blessing or a curse? No one knows. We only have a fragment. Life comes in fragments.'

It so happened that a few weeks later the country engaged in war against a neighbouring country. All the young men of the village were required to join the army. Only the son of the old man was excluded, because he was injured. Once again the people gathered around the old man, crying and screaming because their sons had been taken. There was little chance that they would return. The enemy was strong, and the war would be a losing struggle. They would never see their sons again. 'You were right, old man,' they wept. 'God knows you were right. This proves it. Your son's accident was a blessing. His legs may be broken, but at least he is with you. Our sons are gone forever.' The old man spoke again. 'It is impossible to talk with you. You always draw conclusions. No one knows. Say only this: Your sons had to go to war, and mine did not. No one knows if it is a blessing or a curse. No one is wise enough to know. Only God knows.'

Hold that story in mind as we go along because its significance will soon become apparent.

How great is God?

Christians declare in the Nicene Creed, 'We believe in God the Father Almighty, Maker of heaven and earth.' It is this bold assertion of God's power which leads many to conclude that *prima facie* there is an apparent contradiction between holding to a belief in an all-powerful, all-loving God on the one hand and the fact of suffering which is considered evil on the other. Not surprisingly we hear people speaking of the '*problem* of suffering' or 'the *problem* of evil'.

At the outset it should be said that for the atheist there isn't a problem of suffering in the sense that evil and suffering do not count against his *beliefs*. For the atheist/materialist, suffering is a mere fact of existence, like the redness of red or the wetness of water—it just 'is'. It *may* be a problem for the atheist in that he, like the rest of us, has to cope with the unpleasantness of suffering, but although he may not like it, he can't complain about it because there is no God to complain to. He can no more object to the presence of suffering in the world than he can rail against the presence of mould.

The 'problem of pain' appears to be a difficulty for the believer because of what he affirms about God, namely, that he is good and almighty. The trilemma was originally put forward by Epicurus, 'Is God willing to prevent evil, but not able? Then he is impotent. Is he able but not willing? Then he is malevolent. Is he both able and willing? Whence evil?' Or, in the words of Professor John Hick, 'If God is perfectly loving and good he must wish to abolish evil; if God is all powerful he must be able to abolish evil. But evil exists therefore God cannot be both perfectly good and almighty.'[2]

What might we say to this common objection?

A moment's reflection upon this conundrum soon reveals two things which the trilemma presupposes for it to be effective. The first presupposition is that if God is good and all powerful he must wish to abolish evil *now,* or at least it raises the questions why he did not remove it earlier or why he allowed it to come into being in the first place. The second presupposition is that he must do it in an immediate and total way. But what if it could be shown, however tentatively, that God will not only deal with suffering at some point in the *future,* but that he has *already* taken decisive steps to deal

---

2. John Hick 'An Irenean Theodicy' *Encountering Evil,* S. T. Davies Ed (T and T Clark 1981) pp. 38–52

with it? Then some, but by no means all, of the sting is taken out of the objection.[3]

Easy but false solutions

There are, of course, some simple solutions to the dilemma which essentially involve the removal of one or more elements of belief so it ceases to be a dilemma at all.

One option would be to deny the existence of suffering, viewing it as 'illusory' in some way. This is the position of Theravada Buddhism which considers suffering (*dukkha*) as part of '*Maya*'—belonging to the vale of illusion.[4] Similarly with Christian Science which views 'pain' to be a product of 'the mortal mind.' But this is hardly satisfactory for most people undergoing hardship. One is reminded of the limerick:

There was once a faith healer from Deal
who said although pain is not real,
when I sit on a pin
and I puncture my skin,
I dislike what I imagine I feel!

The second alternative is to deny that God is all-powerful

---

3. It could also be argued that there is a third assumption, namely that God's 'goodness' is reduced to pure benevolence. But the Bible portrays God's goodness as being much richer and deeper than benevolence as it also incorporates righteousness and wisdom. In part, it is the working out of these latter two qualities which account for the presence of evil and suffering in the present, as I will argue.

4. 'Brahman alone is real, the phenomenal world is unreal, or mere illusion' *An Encyclopaedia of Religion*, ed. Vergilius Ferm (The Philosophical Library, 1945), P. 707. For a helpful summary of Eastern Monism's take on suffering and evil see, 'Nirvana is not for Egos' in Os Guinness, *Unspeakable. Facing Up to Evil in an Age of Genocide and Terror* (Harper Collins, 2005).

which is what the Process theologian, David Griffin, does when he states quite unashamedly that his solution is found by 'denying the doctrine of omnipotence fundamental to it'.[5]

Thirdly, there is the denial of God's goodness which is expressed to great effect by Archibald MacLeish in his play, *J. B.*, an updated re-presentation of the story of Job. At various intervals throughout the play there is the haunting refrain, 'If he is God he is not good, if he is good he is not God'. In the play a clergyman tells J. B. that his suffering is caused by the simple fact he is a man, that it is all part of the human condition, to which J. B. responds, 'Yours is the cruellest comfort of all, making the Creator of the Universe the miscreator of mankind, a party to the crimes He punishes.'[6]

The traditional Christian claim, however, is that God is good, almighty, and that evil and suffering are realities to be reckoned with. The 'problem' therefore turns on how to relate these two articles of faith (the goodness and omnipotence of God) to the fact of suffering, without compromising either of these tenets of belief or trivializing human anguish.

Suffering as evil

In turning to consider the question, 'What makes suffering morally reprehensible?' a prior question needs to be addressed: 'Is all suffering evil or is it so only in certain contexts?' Whilst psychologically most pain might be considered to be objectionable, it is not necessarily the case

---

5. David Griffith, 'Creation out of Chaos and the Problem of Evil' in *Encountering Evil*, Edited by Stephen T. Davis (T&T Clark, 1981), p 105
6. Archibald MacLeish, *J.B: A Play in Verse* (Houghton Mifflin, 1958) p 126

that it is morally so, especially if the pain endured is part of means to a recognized good. For example, biologically pain serves as part of the body's defence mechanism preventing further injury by means of say, a reflex action. In some contexts it is morally neutral, like the 'healthy' pain after long exercise, or morally good, as in the case of corrective punishment.

What makes suffering morally objectionable is its occurrence in a form which is wholly negative and apparently devoid of any significant purpose. It is this which lies at the root of so many tormented human cries—'Why should my ten-day-old baby die?' 'Why should such a gifted man be reduced to a mere shell through Alzheimer's?' It is this seeming lack of *purpose* which provides the twist which calls for such pain to be viewed as evil. This is what philosophers refer to as 'dysteleological suffering'.

When we ask the question, 'Why is there suffering?' we could be straining towards one of two things.

First, we could be looking backward for some cause: 'What is the cause of suffering?'—both in terms of an ultimate cause—'Where did it come from in the first place?' or in the more immediate sense, 'What is the cause of this *particular* suffering?' This approach has a distinguished Christian pedigree with advocates such as Augustine,[7] C. S. Lewis[8] and Stephen T. Davis.[9]

---

7. Augustine, '*On Free Will*' and '*Confessions*' VIII, and '*Enchiridion*' ch. IV

8. C. S. Lewis, *The Problem of Pain* (Fountain, 1976)

9. Stephen T Davis, 'Free Will and Evil' in *Encountering Evil,* S. T. Davies, Ed (T and T Clark 1981)

The nature and origin of evil

Within this tradition, a significant place is given to the role of the devil. But even if a much of the moral evil which is to be seen in the world is attributed to such a creature it merely pushes the question of origins one stage back, for it can be asked: 'Where did the devil come from?' 'Surely', it is said, 'if he is a creature made by God then doesn't this make God the author of evil? And if that is the case, then how can God be good?'

The first thing to say is that the Bible has very little, if anything at all, to say about the origin of Satan. Much of what has come into mainstream Christian thinking is the result of the speculation of poets such as John Milton in his '*Paradise Lost*' or Chaucer's '*Canterbury Tales*'. Sometimes claims are made that Bible passages such as Isaiah 14:12–15 are a description of Satan's origin: 'How you have fallen from heaven, O morning star, son of the dawn! You have been cast down to the earth, you who once laid low the nations! You said in your heart, "I will ascend to heaven; I will raise my throne above the stars of God; I will sit enthroned on the mount of assembly, on the utmost heights of the sacred mountain. I will ascend above the tops of the clouds; I will make myself like the Most High." But you are brought down to the grave, to the depths of the pit.' But is this really about the devil? A careful look at the context shows that this passage is referring not to some angelic being but the King of Babylon.[10] One reason for it being linked to Satan is because

---

10. This was the view taken by John Calvin in his commentary on Isaiah, 'How art thou fallen from heaven! Isaiah proceeds with the discourse which he had formerly begun as personating the dead, and concludes that the tyrant differs in

of the way the Latin version of the Bible—the Vulgate—
translated the phrase 'morning star' as 'Lucifer'. However,
it could well be that Isaiah is drawing on a myth which
was current in Babylon itself, in which the 'Bright shiner'
(Hebrew—'heylel'), the name given to the planet Venus, also
called 'son of the dawn' because it rises shortly before the sun,
tried to become King by scaling the mountain ramparts of the
heavenly city, only to be vanquished by the all-conquering

---

no respect from other men, though his object was to lead men to believe that he
was some god. He employs an elegant metaphor, by comparing him to Lucifer,
and calls him the Son of the Dawn; and that on account of his splendour and
brightness with which he shone above others. The exposition of this passage,
which some have given, as if it referred to Satan, has arisen from ignorance; for
the context plainly shows that these statements must be understood in reference
to the king of the Babylonians. But when passages of Scripture are taken up at
random, and no attention is paid to the context, we need not wonder that mistakes
of this kind frequently arise. Yet it was an instance of very gross ignorance, to
imagine that Lucifer was the king of devils, and that the Prophet gave him this
name. But as these inventions have no probability whatever, let us pass by them
as useless fables.' *Calvin's Commentaries, Isaiah*, Translated by William Pringle
(Baker, 1999), p 442. See also, Ronald Youngblood, 'The Fall of Lucifer,' in *The
Way of Wisdom: Essays in Honour of Bruce K. Waltke*, eds. J. I. Packer and
Sven Soderlund [Grand Rapids, MI: Zondervan, 2000], p 171. However, earlier
theologians such as Augustine did identify the 'Bright Shiner' as Satan; 'Isaiah
represents the devil symbolically as the prince of Babylon and apostrophizes him
thus: "How Lucifer has fallen, who used to rise in the morning!" ... he is not to be
supposed to sin from his beginning, when he was created, but from the beginning
of his sin, because it was by his pride that sin first came to be.', Augustine, *The City
of God Against the Pagans*, vol. 3, trans. David S. Wiesen, in the Loeb Classical
Library, ed. G. P. Goold (Cambridge: Harvard University Press, 1988), 486. I
would suggest that the likes of Calvin were guided more by the grammatical-
historical context of Scripture in their interpretation in contrast to Augustine and
Tertullian and are therefore more reliable as guides.

Sun.[11] If that is the case then this picture is taken, reapplied and given a new twist by Isaiah, for now it applies to the King of Babylon. This king is inordinately proud; having aspirations to world domination, but God will ensure that he will fail.

In the Book of Job, the Satan appears as one of the 'sons of God' in the heavenly counsel together with other angels which suggests he is an angelic creature whose business is acting as the chief prosecutor of God's people, seeking their damnation if you like, for that is what the term, 'the Satan' means—the adversary or accuser.[12] But we are still left with trying to gain some understanding as to how such a wicked being came into existence in the first place if, as we read in Genesis, God made everything 'good'.

One fruitful line of thought has been suggested by Augustine and popularized by C. S. Lewis in *Mere Christianity*. This is the idea that 'evil' can't be 'created' as such, because it does not have the kind of substantial existence that 'good' has. Good can exist all by itself, but evil can't. Evil is parasitic on the good in that if there were no good, there would be no evil, but it is possible have good without evil. For example, one could imagine a perfectly good orange and beside it an orange which has gone bad, infected by a fungus. While it is possible to have the good orange without the bad, one cannot have the bad without it being

---

11. See G. B. Caird, *The Language and Imagery of the Bible* (Duckworth, 1980), pp 224–225

12. For a careful consideration of the Book of Job and suffering see, Chapter 8 'Providence and Suffering' in Melvin Tinker, *Intended for Good: The Providence of God* (Inter Varsity Press 2011) pp 113–130

formerly good. Or we may think of blindness as the absence of sight and so as blindness is the departure from sight, so sin is the departure from good. Here, then, evil is more of an 'unmaking' of what is good, a corruption.

Take the case of evil desires; these are simply a mimicking of good desires. Thieves want to possess things which are good in themselves like beautiful possessions. Gluttons desire food which is good in itself—like beef wellington. Adulterers desire that which is good, namely, sex. Even tyrants might want good things for their country—harmony and prosperity. But what makes them evil are the wrong motives which drive them and the wrong means used to get them. When good things don't occupy their rightful place in the way God has ordered his universe, they then become bad. Evil is a disfigurement of the good.

Therefore, if evil is a good thing misappropriated, an 'unmaking 'of the good as it were, then we are perhaps given a clue as to how evil, and indeed the devil, may have originally come about.

Just suppose for a moment that a good, personal being— like an angel—chooses to try and occupy a position that isn't rightly his in God's universe. Then what? Then the choosing—a good thing—becomes a bad thing because of *what* is chosen. When that happens, the act of choosing becomes corrupted and so does the person doing the choosing, it boomerangs back on his character so his will becomes more and more inclined to choosing what is wrong. It makes little sense to ask the question, 'What made the being choose the wrong in the first place', because by definition a choice is just that—a choice. To be 'made' to 'choose' something is a contradiction in terms—it ceases to be a choice, instead it is a compulsion. No, the person simply makes a decision—it is irreducible. Certainly all sorts of factors are taken into account when deciding what to do, but at the end of the day all you can say is that a person *chose*. And so if Satan is a 'fallen angel', then such a fall came about by a simple choice, as did the later fall of human beings.[13]

The Bible portrays a sovereign and totally good God creating a good universe (good in the sense of 'fit for purpose')[14] but we human beings rebelled and that rebellion is now such a part of our make up that we are enmeshed in it (Genesis 1–3). All the suffering we now face turns on this fact, and is in some way related to 'sin', but not all suffering is related to sin in the same way. The Bible centres on how God

---

13. The objection is sometimes raised that if man was originally created 'good' then why did he choose to rebel? Apart from the irreducible nature of the notion of 'choice' as we have discussed, the fact that something is created 'good' does not mean that it is as good as can be. John Calvin even suggested that Adam was created good in this sense but was 'weak, frail and liable to fall'. In his Institutes he writes, 'Therefore Adam could have stood if he wished, seeing that he fell solely by his own will. But it was because his will was capable of being bent to one side or the other, and was not given to constancy to persevere, that he fell so easily.' (Inst. 1.15.8). See Paul Helm, *John Calvin's Ideas* (Oxford University Press, 2006), p 110

14. William Dumbrell comments on the Hebrew word *tob* ('good') as follows: '[While it] has many shades of
meaning, ranging from "useful" to "beautiful" to "valuable", the meaning of the word in any particular case will be conditioned to a large extent by its immediate context. It can certainly mean "aesthetically good" or "ethically good" and need not mean "perfection". We agree with those who suggest that in the context of Genesis 1 the meaning is best taken as "efficient".' William Dumbrell, 'Life and Death in God's Creative Purposes' in B. G. Webb (ed.), *The Ethics of Life and Death*, Lancer, 1990, p 8.

takes action to reverse these terrible effects and their root
cause, which is sin itself

This means that there is a fundamental recognition by
the Christian that the world in which we live is thrown
out of joint at every level and that the price of sin is great
Furthermore suffering in this life is in some measure a
consequence of it. Nevertheless, this is not to say that every
item of suffering is the *immediate* consequence or penalty of
sin. It is patently obvious that many 'good people' do suffer,
and Christians of all people should certainly not expect a
trouble-free life.[15]

While some suffering can be the result of specific sins so
that if one lives a profligate life like that of the 1930s movie
star Errol Flynn dining out on drugs, booze and women,
then you can reasonably expect to die like Errol Flynn—VD
riddled, drug-addicted and with a liver shot to ruin by the age
of 50. But sometimes the consequences of human sin can be
more broadly distributed on the human scene in a way that
does not appear very discriminating such as with war, plague,
and congenital defects.

It is at this point that an objection is raised which goes
something like this: 'If God does care about us and is so
opposed to sin, which is the cause of so much suffering in the
world, why doesn't he intervene and do something about it?'.

This is how the writer, Dorothy L. Sayers, responds to those
kinds of questions in her characteristic forthright way:

---

15. Luke 13:1–5

'Why doesn't God smite this dictator dead?' is a question a little remote from us. Why, madam did he not strike you dumb and imbecile before you uttered that baseless and unkind slander the day before yesterday? Or me, before I behaved with such a cruel lack of consideration to that well-meaning friend? And why sir, did he not cause your hand to rot off at the wrist before you signed your name to that dirty bit of financial trickery? You did not quite mean that? But why not? Your misdeeds and mine are none the less repellent because our opportunities for doing damage are less spectacular than those of some other people. Do you suggest that your doings and mine are too trivial for God to bother about? That cuts both ways; for in that case, it would make precious little difference to his creation if he wiped us both out tomorrow.[16]

In other words, if we want strict and immediate *justice*, then what we are asking for is literally hell, for that is precisely what it would be and life could hardly be lived at all.

Purpose in pain?

In addition to looking backward for an answer to the question, 'Why suffering?' in terms of causation, we could also look forward, and ask: 'What is the *purpose* of suffering?' 'What possible good, if any, could there be in it?' This is what is known as the teleological approach.

This way of looking at the question was in fact taken up by a certain school of psychoanalysis called logotherapy, headed by Viktor Frankl, who himself experienced the horrors of Auschwitz. It was there of all places that he noticed

---

16. Dorothy L Sayers, 'The Triumph of Easter', *Creed or Chaos?* (Methuen, 1954)

the positive way in which some people approached their situation. This observation in turn led him to quote Nietzsche with approval when he said that 'Men and women can endure any amount of suffering so long as they know the why to their existence'. In other words, if that suffering can be placed within some wider context of meaning and purpose, much, but no means all, of the sting is taken out.

There is a story in John 9 which illustrates this point well: the healing of the man born blind: As Jesus and his disciples came across this man, it was the disciples who raised the question: 'Who sinned, this man or his parents?' (vv1-2). They were looking for an answer to this tragic state of affairs in terms of causation linked to a specific sinful action. But Jesus replied in verse 3, 'Neither, but this happened *so that* (*hina*)[17] the work of God may be displayed in his life'. Jesus alters the perspective by focusing upon the divine *purpose* behind the situation, linking it to the creative-redeeming activity of God. Accordingly the man is healed. This is where the main emphasis lies in the New Testament. Many of the early Christians had to face opposition and persecution and needed strength and reassurance to witness to Christ. That mainly came from viewing things within an eternal perspective.[18]

---

17. A purposive clause 'in order that' (*hina*).

18. In the early church John Chrysostom placed the issue of suffering within the wider context of God's Providential purposes, which includes God's use of Satan as an instrument in order to refine his people, 'For as a gold refiner having cast a piece of gold into the furnace allows it to be proved by the fire until such a time as he sees it has become purer: even so God permits the souls of men to be tested by troubles until they become pure and transparent and have reaped much profit from this process of sifting; wherefore this is the greatest species of benefit.'

This comes out in several places. We may think of Romans 5:1–5, 'Therefore, since we have been justified through faith, we have peace with God through our Lord Jesus Christ, through whom we have gained access by faith into this grace in which we now stand. And we boast in the hope of the glory of God. Not only so, but we also glory in our sufferings, because we know that suffering produces perseverance; perseverance, character; and character, hope. And hope does not put us to shame, because God's love has been poured out into our hearts through the Holy Spirit, who has been given to us.' Later in 8:28ff Paul writes, 'And we know that in all things God works for the good of those who love him, who have been called according to his purpose'.[19] But we may

---

With regard to the work of Satan, this is seen as a means used by God to develop and mature the character of believers and so magnify the ministry of the Gospel in the world: 'Nevertheless, though the devil had set so many traps, not only did he not shake the church, but instead made her more brilliant. For during the period when she was not troubled she did not teach the world as effectively as she now does to be patient, to practise self-restraint, to bear trials, to demonstrate steadfast endurance, to scorn the things of the present life, to pay no regards to riches, to laugh at honour, to pay no heed to death, to think lightly of life, to abandon homeland, households, friends, and close relations, to be prepared for all kinds of wounds, to throw oneself against the swords, to consider all the illustrious things of the present life—I am speaking of honour, glories, power and luxury—as more fragile than the flowers of springtime.' Cited in Christopher A. Hall, *Learning Theology with the Church Fathers* (Inter Varsity Press, 2002), pp. 183–205.

19. The purposive nature of suffering has been well put by John Calvin, 'Although the paternal favour and beneficence, as well as the judicial severity of God, is often conspicuous in the whole course of his Providence, yet occasionally as the causes of events are concealed, the thought is apt to rise, that human affairs are whirled about by blind impulse of Fortune ... It is true indeed, that if with sedate and quiet minds we were disposed to learn, the issue would at length make it manifest that the counsel of God was in accordance with the highest reason, that his purpose was either to train his people patience, correct their depraved

want to ask: 'Upon what grounds could Paul or anyone else for that matter, make such a startling claim that God can and will work 'all things for good?'. This brings us to the central act of the Christian faith, namely, the death and resurrection of the God-man, Jesus Christ.

It is at the Cross where we are presented with the paradox running throughout the mysterious relationship between the evil of suffering and God's good purposes. From one point of view, the Cross was the worst thing that could have happened (the murder of the divine Son, so pinpointing forcefully our rebellious attitude towards God). Yet at *the same time* it was the best thing that ever happened (the Divine means of rescuing us). Here we see God taking sin and suffering seriously because he tasted it first hand in his Son, whose suffering physically and spiritually was of a magnitude beyond our comprehension. It was this which shaped the New Testament writers' attitude towards suffering, the belief that the outworkings of what God had achieved by Jesus' death and resurrection *in time* would be brought to completion at *the end of time,* ushering in the new heaven and the new earth.

It is this future dimension which is so important.

If this world were the total story, then suffering would never make sense. There is no righting of wrongs in this world. The good do suffer injustice and the guilty at times get off scot free. It is but 'a tale told by an idiot full of sound and fury'.

---

affections, tame their wantonness, insure them to self-denial; or on the other hand to cast down the proud, defeat the craftiness of the ungodly and frustrate all their schemes.' *Institutes*, Book One Chapter 17 (Eerdmans 1983)

But the Bible says that the best is yet to come, a day when every tear will be wiped away from our eyes by God himself and suffering and death will be no more.[20]

This brings us back to the parable of the woodcutter with which we began.

It is very difficult for us to pronounce on what is ultimately good or bad for us in life because we only have a small slice of the picture. It may be that what we are undergoing at the moment will not only be for our good (making us into better people) but other people's good too. Sometimes that good will be seen in this life, but much will not be seen until the next life.

While it is sometimes said that Christians believe that there are no such things as 'accidents' only 'God incidents', so that every single event (including one's involving suffering and evil) has meaning within the great scheme of things, the real significance and purpose of some events may not be seen in this life at all, but only in eternity, which, after all, is the fuller setting of God's big picture.

How might we understand how this works out? Here is a simple illustration. It is said that Persian carpets are made on a large frame. On one side of the frame stand the mother

---

20. Dr Timothy Keller refers to the climax of *The Lord of the Rings* to illustrate this liberating Christian truth. Sam Gamgee discovers that his friend Gandalf is not dead (as he thought) but is alive. He cries, 'I thought you were dead! But then I thought I was dead myself! Is everything sad going to come untrue?' Keller goes on to remark, 'The answer of Christianity is—yes. Eventually everything sad is going to come untrue and it will somehow be *greater* for having once been broken and lost.' Timothy Keller, *The Reason for God: Belief in an Age of Scepticism* (Riverhead Books, 2008) p 33

and her children, placing different coloured threads into the framework, sometimes randomly, sometimes thoughtfully. On the other side of the frame out of sight stands the father of the family. He is the master carpet weaver who takes all of these threads and weaves them into a rich pattern of *his* design. As the work is in progress, all that the family can see from their side of the frame are rough patterns, and in some cases, no pattern at all. But from the father's side he knows exactly what he is doing with the threads his family put into the frame. When the carpet is completed the father turns the finished product around for all to see and hopefully receives their approval of a job well done. Might not God, the Heavenly Father, be likened to the master weaver who takes each thread that we place into the framework of our lives only to weave them into a pattern which is of his design? The main difference being, of course, is that from the beginning God knows what those threads are and where they will be placed on 'our' side of the frame. However, it is the 'other' side of the frame, eternity if you will, which provides the lasting context in which ultimate significance is derived. It is in the new heaven and the new earth that we will be able to declare that our God has done all things well. We hold to that now by faith, then it will give way to sight.[21]

How can Christians have this more creative attitude towards suffering, believing that although it is sometimes hard to bear by God's grace, nothing is ever wasted and with the apostle Paul they can say, 'In all things God works to the

---

21. For a presentation of this argument, see Melvin Tinker, *Why Do Bad Things Happen to Good People?* (Christian Focus, 2009).

good for those who love him? (Romans 8:28).[22] It is because of the cross of Christ and what followed—the resurrection.

I guess that if we had been there on that first Good Friday and saw Jesus who had done so many wonderful things suffering as he did we might have said 'Why is God allowing this? It serves no purpose. Why didn't he allow Jesus to live a while longer and heal a few more people?' But of course, unbeknown to us at the time (but revealed later on), God was taking the worse event ever—the murder of the Son of God—and at the same time working through it the best thing ever—the means of our salvation. We would have been there at one point in the divine story, an obscure point. But then three days later there was the resurrection. This was the next chapter in the story which declared that death wasn't the end, something else was happening on that cross so that for all who trust in Christ they too can have a certain assurance that neither death nor suffering will have the last word, but rather God, when he creates a new heaven and a new earth for a new people with new non-suffering bodies to occupy it (Revelation 21).

Let me give an example of the difference belief in the resurrection makes when facing almost unbearable calamity.

Professor J N D Anderson went to Cambridge University in the 1930s where he met his future wife. Here he became very active in the student evangelical movement of the day, the Cambridge Inter Collegiate Christian Union (CICCU). After

---

22. The danger is that such a verse can be trotted out by Christians such that it becomes an insensitive cliché. There are instances of human suffering which are so grotesque and indescribable that it is difficult to envisage any 'good' being associated with them. See for example Elie Wiesel's harrowing account of his experiences in Auschwitz in his book *Night*.

graduating he went to Egypt as a missionary where he learnt Arabic. During the Second World War he was recruited by British Intelligence. After the war he returned to Britain and eventually become Professor of Oriental Laws and Director of the Institute for Advanced legal Studies at the University of London. He wrote many fine Christian books, including a best seller booklet—'The Evidence for the Resurrection—a lawyer examines the evidence' which God has used to bring a countless number of people to a saving faith in Christ. He was eventually given a knighthood by the Queen. Sir Norman Anderson and his wife had three children, all fine Christians. His first daughter became a medical missionary in what was then the Belgian Congo (present day Zaire). During the violence that erupted there during the Simba uprising, she was gang raped. She came home and eventually went to California to do some advance study in medicine with the intention of returning to the Congo. But while there, she tripped, fell down some stairs and drowned in her own spittle. The second daughter died in circumstances scarcely less bizarre.

Their only son, Hugh was a brilliant student at Cambridge University gaining a distinguished First and even then was being tipped as a future Prime Minister of Great Britain. However, at the tender age of 21 he died of brain cancer.

How do you deal with experiences like that with tragedy piled upon tragedy? This is what Sir Norman said on a broadcast on the BBC a few days after his son had died. After explaining why he himself was convinced that God raised Jesus from the dead, he said, 'On this I am prepared to stake my life. In this faith my son died, after saying, "I'm drawing near my Lord." I am convinced that he was not mistaken.'

When God came into the world, he didn't smile at suffering like a Buddha—he dealt with it by healing the sick, opening the eyes of the blind and raising the dead. He met real physical needs. But such deeds also acted as 'parables' pointing to what God wants to do with our deeper spiritual needs which underlie all our social and physical problems, namely our sin. He wants to clear up our spiritual blindness our spiritual deafness and bring us back into a relationship with himself, a relationship of love. All of us have to go through this painful world and I would rather go through it with Jesus than without him.

Wherever we look in the New Testament we cannot fail to be struck by the wonderful truth that the God whom we see in Jesus Christ is no remote God. He was not willing only to get his hands dirty; he was willing for them to be pierced for the sake of those who did it. Here again are some wise words of Dorothy L Sayers:

> For whatever reason God chose to make man as he is— limited and suffering and subject to sorrows and death—He had the honesty and the courage to take His own medicine. Whatever game He is playing with His creation, He has kept His own rules and played fair. He has Himself gone through the whole of human experience, from the trivial irritations of family life and lack of money to the worst horrors, pain, humiliation, defeat, despair and death. He was born in poverty and died in disgrace and felt it was all worthwhile.[23]

No other religion speaks of God like that!

---

23. Dorothy L Sayers 'The Greatest Drama Ever Staged' in *Creed or Chaos*

5

If God is Sovereign, How can we be free?

Introduction

A highly significant and yet often overlooked verse in Scripture is Deuteronomy 29:29 where Moses declares: 'The secret things belong to the Lord our God, but the things revealed belong to us and to our children forever, that we may follow all the words of his law.' It does seem a natural human tendency to supplement what we think is lacking in the Bible (the 'secret things') because we feel uncomfortable with what we consider to be gaps in our knowledge. However, 'Part of what it means to be "biblical" ... is being prepared to live with scriptural gaps.'[1] Peter Bolt wisely cautions: 'If there is a gap in the biblical material, instead of rushing to fill it from elsewhere, it is important to ask how the Bible uses it in communicating its main message. The answer, most likely,

---

1. Peter Bolt, 'Defeat of the Evil Powers' in *Christ's Victory over Evil*, Ed. Peter Bolt (Apollos, 2009) p 48

will be that the gap draws the hearer in more tightly to the central message of the Scriptures.'[2] This particularly needs to be born in mind as we think about the relationship between God's sovereignty and human freedom. Here the temptation will be to fill in the gaps with our own speculation on the one hand or distort Scripture by emphasizing one element at the expense of another on the other.

We need to be mindful of the context of the words of Moses, namely, God's self-revelation to his people who are about to enter the land of promise, a revelation designed to enable them to live under his rule by obedient faith. The premise is that God has given *sufficient* (but not exhaustive) knowledge in his Word to do this (Deuteronomy 8:3). If that was the case with his people under the Old Covenant, how much more so with his people in the light of the full revelation of Christ in the New?[3]

The opening line of one of the great Christian Creeds, the Nicene creed, boldly states that Christians believe in 'One God, the Father *Almighty*.' This is the teaching that the God of the Bible is far bigger than we often imagine him to be. He is Sovereign over every twist and turn of existence whilst at the same time recognizing that human beings are responsible for what they do. The biblical belief is that God superintends and overrules all events—including human choices—in order to fulfil a purpose of his own design. This is something the Bible presents with no explanation as to *how* God does this, it

---

2. Ibid., p 48
3. Hebrews 3:7–19

simply conveys the fact *that* he does it, as well as pointing to some of the comforting implications we are to draw.[4]

The Latin word to describe God the Father as 'Almighty' is *'omnipotens'* from which we get our word 'Omnipotent'—all powerful. The Greek word is *'pantokrator'* which was used in the Greek translation of the Old Testament (LXX) to render the Hebrew phrase, 'Lord of Hosts'—meaning that God is sovereign ruler of the universe. Our word 'sovereign' comes from the Latin *superanitas* literally meaning 'aboveness'.[5] God has not only *made* the heaven and the earth—'all things visible and invisible', as the Creed puts it—he sovereignly *rules* over those things too, right down to the 'fall of a sparrow' (Matthew 10:29-31).

How, then, are we to begin to understand the relationship between the sovereignty of God over the world and the responsibility of human beings, made in his image acting as moral agents in a way which is in line with the biblical witness? To help us move towards answering this question we shall draw on the Scriptural witness itself and also

---

4. See Melvin Tinker, *Intended for Good—the Providence of God* (Inter Varsity Press, 2012). Also, Stephen N Williams: 'The notion of providence encapsulates the conviction that God sustains the world that he has created and directs it to its appointed destiny. Belief in God's providence evokes not only humility and wonder, but also gratitude and trust, for believers know God as Father and believe that "in all things God works for the good of those who love him, who have been called according to his purpose" (Romans 8:28, NIV)' in 'Providence', *The New Dictionary Of Biblical theology* (Inter Varsity Press, 2000), p 711

5. 'It is this aboveness that is the determining factor of his [God's] authority over us. We are subject to him, but he is subject to no-one, and so to know him is to know the one who ultimately governs and controls our lives.' Gerald Bray, *Yours is the Kingdom—A Systematic Theology of the Lord's Prayer* (Inter Varsity Press, 2007), p 40

look at a model taken from the field of mechanistic brain science which, hopefully, provides us with some insight into the nature of this relationship without falling prey to the reductionist tendencies mentioned earlier of trying to fill in the gaps in our knowledge.

Two Propositions

We begin by formulating two propositions or 'givens' which arise inductively out of Scripture's own testimony:

1. God is absolutely sovereign but his sovereignty never functions in the Bible to reduce, minimize or negate human responsibility.

2. Human beings are responsible agents—they make morally significant choices. But human responsibility never functions in the Bible to diminish God's sovereignty or to make God absolutely contingent.[6]

The name given to the position which holds these two propositions together in a state of tension is *compatibilism*.

Back to the Bible

Here are a handful of selected passages (out of scores which could be given properly viewed in their wider context) which clearly teach one or other of the two propositions, in some cases both at one and the same time.[7]

---

6. I follow here D.A. Carson, 'The Mystery of Providence' as argued in *How Long O Lord?* (Inter Varsity Press, 1990) Chapter 11 'The Mystery of Providence' pp 199–228. See also his fuller treatment, *Divine Sovereignty and Human Responsibility: Biblical Perspectives in Tension* (Marshal, Morgan and Scott, 1981).

7. What follows is not simple 'proof texting' which can involve taking a text out of its wider context to prove a theological point. I am presenting here what

God's absolute sovereignty

Proverbs 16:4: 'The LORD [Yahweh] works out everything for his own ends—even the wicked for the day of disaster.' This means that even the affairs and plans of men are known to him and will be used by him to serve his good purpose. God is never to be caught napping at any point or found off guard such that he is ever forced to say, 'I didn't see that one coming! I had better revert to plan B. But if that gets messed up I will go on to plan C and work my way down.' No, his plans are never ultimately stymied by our cleverness or cunning, even wicked people come under his sovereign sway. No matter how powerful a person is, they too do not escape his eternal decrees—Proverbs 21:1: 'The king's heart is in the hand of the LORD; he directs it like a watercourse wherever he pleases.' Even the hearts of the world's 'movers and shakers' aren't 'no go' areas for God.

Human Responsibility

Ezekiel 18:30–32: 'Therefore, you Israelites, I will judge each of you according to your own ways, declares the Sovereign Lord. Repent! Turn away from all your offenses; then sin will not be your downfall. Rid yourselves of all the offenses you have committed, and get a new heart and a new spirit. Why will

---

Professor Paul Helm calls 'theological one-liners': 'One liners are short statements about God, or even parenthetical clauses, that, although they first occur on some particular occasion, in some context, nevertheless transcend that occasion and context. They are statements which, even when they are de-dramatized, express permanent truths about God, truths which transcend both actions of the divine drama and conversations between God and man.'—in 'Vanhoozer V—Don't Forget the Oneliners,' 2010—http://paulhelmsdeep.blogspot.

you die, people of Israel? For I take no pleasure in the death
of anyone, declares the Sovereign Lord. Repent and live!'

Romans 10:9–11: 'If you declare with your mouth, "Jesus is
Lord," and believe in your heart that God raised him from
the dead, you will be saved. For it is with your heart that you
believe and are justified, and it is with your mouth that you
profess your faith and are saved. As Scripture says, "Anyone
who believes in him will never be put to shame."'

Here human beings are presented as responsible moral
agents addressed by God who are expected to respond in
appropriate ways, namely, in repentance and faith.

God's sovereignty *and* human responsibility.
There are also texts which position both truths side by side.

Proverbs 16:9: 'In his heart a man plan's his course [human
responsibility] but the LORD determines his steps [divine
sovereignty]'.

From the lips of Jesus we hear these words:

I praise you, Father, Lord of heaven and earth, because
you have hidden these things from the wise and learned, and
revealed them to little children. Yes, Father, for this is what you
were pleased to do. All things have been committed to me by
my Father. No one knows the Son except the Father, and no
one knows the Father except the Son and those to whom the
Son chooses to reveal him [divine sovereignty]. Come to me,
all you who are weary and burdened, and I will give you rest.
Take my yoke upon you and learn from me, for I am gentle and
humble in heart, and you will find rest for your souls. For my

yoke is easy and my burden is light. [human responsibility]—
Matthew 11: 25–30.

Since the Bible is at ease in putting both standpoints together without any hint of embarrassment or need for an explanation, so should we be.

Let's focus on one passage as a case example which illustrates the importance of holding to both beliefs equally, namely, the apostle Peter's Pentecost speech as recorded in Acts 2:22ff.

In Acts 2:22ff the apostle Peter says, 'Men of Israel. Listen to this: Jesus of Nazareth was a man accredited by God to you by miracles, wonders and signs, which God did among you through him, as you yourselves know. *This man was handed over to you by God's set purpose and foreknowledge; and you, with the help of wicked men, put him to death by nailing him to the cross.* But God raised him from the dead …'

Here we have the Biblical balance.

A moment's thought reveals that the Christian message itself, the Gospel, is totally dependent upon affirming both these truths.

Just think about it.

If the initiative to kill Jesus lay *solely* with the Jewish leaders and the Romans then that means God simply came in at the last minute to snatch triumph from the jaws of defeat. Then the cross was *not* his plan and purpose, the very reason why he sent his Son into the world. That is totally unthinkable for then Peter could not say it was according to 'God's set purpose'.

If, however, God so manoeuvred events so that all the
human agents—Judas, Pilate, the Chief priests and people
were non-responsible puppets, then it makes no sense for
Peter to call upon the people to repent for what they have
done. How can they repent for what they were 'forced' to
do, as a puppet is 'forced' to move at the bidding of the
strings pulled by the puppet master? They can't unless they
made the choices themselves. To deny human responsibility
would also mean that there was no sin for which Jesus came
to die because in order to be accused of sin you have to be
responsible for sinning! The Bible will not have that either.
Instead, we have the properly balanced picture: God was
sovereignly at work in the death of Jesus; human beings were
wicked in putting him to death, even as they accomplished
the Father's will in doing so, and God remains perfectly
good. As the Puritan Thomas Watson put it, 'Herein is God's
wisdom, that the sins of men carry on his work, yet he has no
hand in them'.[8]

---

8. Commenting on God's use of wicked Assyria to bring about his purposes in
Isaiah 10, Watson writes, 'The wisdom of God is seen in this—that the sins of men
shall carry on God's work; yet He Himself should have no hand in their sin. The
Lord permits sin—but does not approve it. He has a hand in the action in which
sin is—but not in the sin of the action. As in the crucifying of Christ, so far as it
was a natural action, God concurred; if He had not given the Jews life and breath,
they could not have done it; but as it was a sinful action, so God abhorred it. A
musician plays upon a viol which is out of tune; the musician is the cause of the
sound—but the jarring and discord is from the viol itself. Just so, men's natural
motion is from God, but their sinful motion is from themselves. When a man
rides on a lame horse, his riding is the cause why the horse goes, but the lameness
is from the horse itself. Herein is God's wisdom—that the sins of men carry on His
work, yet He has no hand in them!' Thomas Watson *A Body of Divinity*, Chapter 7
http://www.shortercatechism.com/resources/watson/wsc_wa_004_e.html

Both pitfalls are avoided by holding propositions 1 and 2 together. They may not be capable of satisfactory resolution in our finite minds, but this does not preclude them from finding resolution in God's mind (Isaiah 55:4).

In our natural inquisitiveness we may want to ask: 'How can this be so?' It is at this point we need to be careful that we don't transgress the principle laid down in Deuteronomy 29:29 and seek to fill the gaps in a non-theological way. The warning of Donald Macleod is worth heeding, 'There are many objections to this doctrine and most of them are philosophical rather than theological. Almost all of them are of this form: How do you reconcile election with this or that? How do you reconcile divine fore-ordination with human responsibility? How do you reconcile election and reprobation with the free offer of the Gospel? Any answer would also be philosophical. There is no theological (that is, revealed, biblical) solution to that dilemma. It is a problem of reconciling two equally important truths, but there is no biblical revelation of the solution to the problem.'[9]

How does God's will and purpose relate to our will and purpose in such a way that he overrules and we are still responsible? The short answer is: no one knows.

Clarifying Concepts

Freedom of the will.

This is a difficult concept to define. However, given what we have seen so far about God's sovereignty we can be confident

---

9. Donald Macleod, *A Faith to Live By* (Mentor—Christian Focus Publications, 1998), p 50

in claiming that it can't be 'absolute power to the contrary', such that our choices curtail God's choices since this would undermine proposition 1. However, as we have seen, the Bible (let alone our own experience) presents us with people making significant choices. The decisions people make arise out of the sort of people they *are,* which in turn shape the people they are to become. The Bible presents us as fallen creatures and so we make fallen choices, choices skewed towards sin.[10] We do not have *absolute* moral autonomy. In short, people simply do what they want to do.[11] This understanding of freedom is known as 'voluntarism' or 'freedom of inclination' a position associated with the great 18th-century American theologian, Jonathan Edwards, although the same thought can be traced back to St Augustine (AD 354–430). Sam Storms helpfully defines the 'Augustinian/ Edwardsian' view of human freedom as 'The ability to act according to his inclination and desires without being compelled to do otherwise by something or someone external

---

10. The Biblical diagnosis of the human condition is well summarised by David in Psalm 51: 'Surely I was sinful at birth, sinful from the time my mother conceived me.' The very core of our personality is twisted by sin. We emerge into the world as damaged goods. This assessment is not restricted to the Bible, the great Enlightenment think, Immanuel Kant said 'Man is a creature of warped wood'.

11. John Piper makes some helpful distinctions at this point: he says when speaking of people having 'free will they mean, 'Our will is free if our preferences and our choices are really our own in such a way that we can justly be held responsible for whether they are good or bad.' But when we take into account what the Bible says about our fallen human nature, there is a different understanding: 'We have free will if we are ultimately or decisively self-determining, and the only preferences and choices that we can be held accountable for are ones that are ultimately or decisively self-determined.' http://www.desiringgod.org/articles/a-beginner-s-guide-to-free-will.

to himself.'[12] In other words we are free to *do* what we desire but we are not free *in* what we desire.

There is quite a different understanding of free will referred to as 'libertarian'. William Hasker, one of the leading advocates of this position, defines it as follows: 'An agent is free with respect to a given action at a given time if at that time it is within the agent's power to perform the action and also in the agent's power to refrain from the action.'[13]

In its more extreme form this is promoted by the movement known as 'Open Theism': 'God's decision to create a cosmos that was capable of love and that was, therefore, populated with free agents was also a decision to create and govern a world he could not unilaterally control ... What it means for God to give agents some degree of morally responsible say-so over what comes to pass is that God's say-so will not unilaterally determine all that comes to pass.'[14]

This is not the place to engage in a full critique of the libertarian view nor of 'Open Theism',[15] but the basic presupposition of libertarianism, that we must be able to act to the contrary to be truly free, is far from proven as demonstrated by Roger Nicole: 'Just about everyone agrees that in heaven there will be no more danger of apostasy. Does this mean that in glory men will be deprived of that freedom

---

12. Sam Storms, *Chosen for Life* (Crossway, 2007), pp. 59–63.

13. William Hasker, 'A Philosophical Perspective', in Pinnock *et al.*, *The Openness of God: A Biblical Challenge to the Traditional Understanding of God* (Inter Varsity Press, 1994), pp. 136–137).

14. Gregory Boyd. in *Four Views on Divine Providence*, ed. Stanley N. Gundry (Zondervan, 2011) p 190

15. See the appendix in Melvin Tinker *Intended for Good* for such a critique.

which constitutes the distinguishing character of humanity, the gift that stands so high that even the sovereign purpose of God must be viewed subordinate to it? Surely not. But if in glory perseverance is not inconsistent with freedom, why should it be thought incompatible on earth?'[16] Why indeed!

It would appear that in terms of a faithful representation of key biblical texts, as well as the overall shape of the Bible's theology concerning God and human beings, the compatibilist position which embraces a voluntarist notion of human freedom is the most satisfying.

Divine Sovereignty

This is the belief that God stands behind all events, great and small, but does not relate to all events in the same way. God is good and morally perfect and so the way he relates to good and evil events in the world is asymmetrical. This means that God stands behind good in such a way that all good can ultimately be attributed to him, but he stands behind evil in such a way that the evil is accredited to secondary causes and agents without escaping his rule and purpose.[17]

God's nature

In Scripture God is consistently portrayed as transcendent, yet personal. If God were only transcendent (and so sovereign) the result would be fatalism (whatever is going to

---

16. 'Some comments on Hebrews 6:4–6 and the Doctrine of the Perseverance of God with the Saints', in G. Hawthorne (ed.), *Current Issues in Biblical and Patristic Interpretation* (Eerdmans, 1975), p. 357, cited by D. A. Carson in *Divine Sovereignty and Human Responsibility Biblical Perspectives in Tension* (Marshal, Morgan and Scott, 1981), p. 208).

17. D.A. Carson, *How Long O Lord*, p 213

happen is going to happen regardless of anything we might decide). If he were only personal but lacking transcendence and omnipotence he would not be trustworthy, things not only could but *would* get out of hand because circumstances might arise which God did not take into account and so stymie his plans. Scripture presents God as both personal and transcendent. He is God-in-relationship. This appears over and over again in the way God deals with his people. And so we read, "'Abraham believe God and it was credited to him as righteousness," and he was called God's friend.' (James 2:23). Trust in God's promises personally revealed to Abraham is the basis of this relationship which issues in friendship.

Together these three affirmations form the essential theological matrix in which we are to view God's sovereignty and human responsibility.

A helpful summary of what we have been looking at so far is provided by S. N. Williams:

> The history of theology is littered with attempts to harmonize these and other biblical data, and even the very broad description of God's government set out above will be judged by some to be misleading and tendentious. But a comprehensive resolution is not necessary. Biblical theology is thoroughly practical; it emphasizes the application of its various truths to life more than their systematic relation to each other. The Christian's practice of adoration, trust, obedience, repentance, faith and perseverance does not depend on an understanding of how different theological ideas are to be woven together. Further, despite the perplexities involved, the dominant impression imparted by Scripture is that of a rich, if systematically elusive, coherence, not of a dismaying

problem. God understands everything that is happening and directs history to its destiny with literally matchless power. The appearance of his actions varies according to their purpose and the relationships involved; he decides to act before he sees or when he sees or whatever he sees or according to what he sees, and in this respect is portrayed as the living and personal God that he is. But he is not caught out in ignorance or error, or prevented by human action from carrying out what he has determined, or manipulated by human entreaty into doing the unwise, the unjust or the unholy, and in this respect he is portrayed as the good and powerful God that he is.[18]

Stepping Back—the Super Scientist

I now want to look at a way of understanding the relation between human decision making and what is called 'determinism' which I have found to be particularly helpful. It certainly requires a fair amount of thinking through. If you find it helpful too, all well and good. If not, don't worry, the biblical case just presented is all you need!

The model I am referring to was originally proposed by the late Professor Donald MacKay, a Christian brain scientist who led a research unit at Keele University.[19]

Imagine, he argues, that there is a super-scientist who through some amazing technology has the ability to describe completely, with no informational gaps, the state of our brain, as well as being able to take into account all possible influences upon that brain. In principle he would be able

---

18. Op cit., p 714

19. See D.M MacKay, 'What determines my choice' in *The Open Mind and Other Essays*, Ed. Melvin Tinker (Inter Varsity Press, 1988) pp 54–65

to predict with infallible accuracy the choices we would make at some point in the near future. It is proposed that the relationship between our conscious experience and the mechanism of the brain is that whatever we experience— 'seeing', 'thinking', 'believing', 'willing', etc. would show up in the physical state of the brain. Accordingly, there is the 'I story'—what we experience as a conscious agent making decisions, and the 'Brain story'—the physical state of our brain—which a super-scientist observer could 'read'.

Theoretically, such a super-scientist could provide a complete description of the state of our brain and so predict in the near future what the 'I story' will be, the choices we will make, beliefs we will hold, and so on.

Furthermore, supposing, for the sake of argument, that our brains were *physically* determined, running in the same way that any other part of our body runs (like the breathing system or the circulatory system); would that mean that we are *metaphysically* determined, such that our 'freedom of choice' is illusory—so we *have* to make the decision we eventually make? To see whether or not this is so the following logical test can be applied, namely, 'Is there a prediction which exists of what someone is going to choose to do which will be fulfilled whether the person making the decision believes the prediction or not if told about it?' That is, is there a prediction which will have an *unconditional claim* to A's assent ('A' being the moral agent in question), such that he would be correct to believe the prediction and in error not to believe it? Or to put it another way, is that predicted decision inevitable for *that person and everyone else* if only he knew it?

When we talk about an 'inevitable event' we mean
something like predicting when the sun will rise tomorrow.
From what we know of the way the solar system works we
are able to predict with pinpoint accuracy when the sun will
appear in the sky and at what point. Allowing for things
carrying on as normal, in this instance it *would* be correct
for *everyone* to believe, and in error not to believe, such
a prediction. But does it work like that when it comes to
decisions *human beings* are going to make in the future? As
we shall see, it does not.

Supposing our super-scientist makes his prediction that
Fred will propose to Susan next Sunday. He has taken
into account all possible factors which are shaping Fred's
thoughts, which show up in the state of his brain (what
MacKay calls the 'Brain Story'). He makes this prediction and
does not show it to Fred. However, he shows the prediction
to his research team. Next Sunday, lo and behold, Fred
proposes to Susan just as the scientist predicted. Does this
mean that the choice was inevitable for Fred if only *he* knew
it? Not at all. Strange thought it may seem, the validity of the
prediction is totally dependent upon A *not* believing it, for
it is a description of Fred's brain state in which he doesn't
believe it.

But supposing instead that the prediction is shown to Fred
before Sunday. Would he have to believe it as inevitable for
him? No, for then he would be in *error* to believe it, for it is a
description of Fred *not* believing it and so would be rendered
invalid for everyone! The reason for this is that the prediction
becomes out of date the moment it has been shown to Fred.

The situation is logically relative, that is, from the

standpoint of the observer Fred's future is totally predictable and in that sense 'inevitable'—inevitable from the standpoint of a detached observer. But from the standpoint of the one who really matters, Fred, it is not inevitable for him. The outcome is open *for him* until he makes up his mind.

But supposing we modify the description so that it allows for Fred believing it. Does that make any difference? Not really. For then Fred would be right to believe it but he would *not* be in error to disbelieve it, since the prediction is designed to be accurate only if Fred *chooses* to believe it. In other words, the choice is still up *to him.*

Summary.

Paradoxically, it would be self-contradictory for you to believe certain things that a detached observer can correctly say (behind your back) about your future. It is not that what he says is false, but that for *you* it is nonsense. It would not be possible for you to be the person he is describing if you were to believe his prediction of a future choice you have not yet made. No prediction of a future decision you have not yet made can exist which is binding upon *you* whether you like it or not, if only you knew it. No matter how predictable it may be for *others*, a normal choice is still up to you. This position is referred to as 'logical indeterminism'.

Transferring the model to the sphere of divine sovereignty/human responsibility

Let's see what happens when this idea is applied to how God relates to human beings and the issue of moral responsibility.

God is all knowing. Known to him are *all* the choices

we will make and could possibly make.[20] But while such a description of our future choices are completely known to God, they are not binding upon us as inevitable if only *we knew them* such that they demand our unconditional assent, for they are descriptions of us not believing them. In other words, no description exists of our future decisions even known to God which lay claim to our unconditional assent.

Case study—Judas (John 13:18-30)

Let's see how this might apply to the case of Judas Iscariot.

Judas's betrayal is portrayed as fulfilling prophecy (Psalm 41:9) and so being foreordained, v18: 'This is to fulfil this passage of Scripture: "He who shared my bread has turned against me."' It is *also* seen as a result of Satan's activity, v27: 'As soon as Judas took the bread, Satan entered into him'. What is more it is a matter of personal choice: 'Do what *you* are about to do', v28. Although the prophecy is couched in general terms, Jesus sees this as specifically applicable to Judas—v26.

Bearing in mind our discussion about predictions of people making future decisions, we can understand why biblical prophecy is of an opaque nature, lacking certain content specifications.

Supposing that Psalm 41:9, as quoted in John 13:18, had

---

20. Philosophers break down God's knowledge into essentially two categories, 'Natural Knowledge' whereby God knows all necessary truth and all possibilities of what 'could happen' (cf Matthew 11: 21) and 'Free knowledge' those things which God has freely planned to bring to pass. Some argue for a third form of knowledge called 'middle—knowledge' a position known as 'Molinism' named after it original proponent the Jesuit theologian, Luis de Molina.

originally run something like this, 'In around 1,000 years' time there will be a man called Judas Iscariot who will be born in Palestine. He will become a member of the inner group of Jesus of Nazareth. He will betray him to his enemies and afterwards in an act of despair commit suicide.' Now try and imagine what might happen 1,000 years later as Judas Iscariot comes across this detailed predictive prophecy. What would you do if you had been in his shoes under such conditions? One could believe it and so carry it out (although psychologically it would be difficult to envisage this happening). Would Judas having in his hand such a prophecy absolve him of all moral responsibility? Not on the basis of MacKay's model outlined above. Other options would have been open to him. He could have chosen not to believe it and decided to be loyal to Jesus. He could have chosen to emigrate to Egypt or some other such place so that he would not be mixed up in an act of betrayal. Following our earlier argument through, such a description would not have an *unconditional claim* to Judas's assent.

Human responsibility is preserved by such a model. But so is God's sovereignty by prophecy being couched in the way it is.

The form prophecies come to us in the Bible lack the sort of specificity which would give them the character of predictive descriptions of future choices. Instead they are couched in more general terms but with enough detail for an identification to be made retrospectively after the event has taken place and so to pronounce that prophecy has been fulfilled. However, known to *God* is the exact detailed specification of the prophecy thus ensuring that his eternal decrees are fulfilled while ensuring human personal responsibility.[21]

The same principle applies to us all. God by virtue of being all-knowing eternally knows all that we will think, say and do and yet this does not absolve us of responsibility, we still make decisions—some good, some bad, some indifferent and they are truly *our* choices for which we are accountable.

Conclusion

To be true to Scripture we must hold to both the belief in divine sovereignty, the God who works 'all things according to the counsel if his will', and human freedom in a voluntarist sense, such that we do make significant choices and are responsible for those choices.

Perhaps the most fitting words to describe the appropriate Christian's attitude towards these key twin beliefs are those of Charles Haddon Spurgeon:

> It is a difficult task to show the meeting place of the purpose of God and the free agency of man. One thing is quite clear; we are not to deny either of them, for they are both facts. It is a fact that God has purposed all things both great and little; neither will anything happen but according to his eternal purpose and decree. It is also a sure and certain fact that often times events hang upon the choice of men. Now how these two things can both be true I cannot tell you, neither probably after long debate could the wisest men in heaven tell you, not even with the assistance of cherubim and seraphim ... They are two

---

21. See C. G. Tinker, 'God's Foreknowledge and Prophecy: a Case Study in Logical Indeterminism and Compatibilism' in *Churchman* 118/1, 2006.

facts that run side by side, like parallel lines ... Can you not believe them both? And is not the space between them a very convenient place to kneel in, adoring and worshipping him whom you cannot understand?

6

What are we to make of 'the demonic'?

Introduction

In his book, *The Screwtape Letters*, in which a senior devil corresponds with a junior devil on how to deter a man from becoming a Christian, C. S. Lewis writes in his preface:

> There are two equal and opposite errors into which our race can fall about the devils. One is to disbelieve in their existence. The other is to believe, and to feel an excessive and unhealthy interest in them.

There is little doubt that both extremes are to be found within today's church. There are those Christians who may not be seeing 'reds under the bed' as many were claiming at the height of the Cold War, but do seem to be seeing 'devils under the beds' so that it is not possible to have a cold in peace without it being construed as some spiritual attack.[1] On the other hand, there are those who have surrendered to the dominant mindset produced by the Enlightenment which on *a priori* grounds rules out all things supernatural as a matter of course. It would seem that a careful reading of the Bible would call down a plague on both houses.

The purpose of this chapter is to draw attention to some of the main points of what the Bible has to say about being aware of the spiritual 'underworld',[2] and especially to think about what is referred to as demon possession.

At the outset it should be noted that Bible does not use the term 'demon possession'. It speaks of people being 'demonized' (Matthew 12:22)—usually rendered as a noun—'demoniac'; having or being with an unclean spirit (Mark 1:23). On one occasion Jesus was accused of 'having Beelzebul'—Mark 3:22. The term 'possession' is an English translation and not a strict one. But we shall use it as a form of short hand for the phenomenon of having a demonic spirit.

Getting the Perspective right

Let's begin by trying to gain some kind of perspective on the subject by first noting that reference to demon possession is

---

1. J W. Woodberry speaks of those whose 'involvement with the demons has so monopolised their time that they have lost balance in other areas of their Christian life', 'Power and Blessing', in Van Engen, Whiteman and Woodberry, *Paradigm Shifts in Christian Witness* (Orbis, 2008), p. 96

2. For a clear and popular introduction to this subject, see Peter Bolt, *Living with the Underworld* (Matthias Media, 2007).

relatively rare in the Bible. What is more, where you might expect it to be found, it is notably absent.[3]

In the Old Testament the phenomenon is only alluded to with regards to one individual, namely, King Saul in 1 Samuel 16:23 and 18:10 'The next day an evil spirit from God came forcefully on Saul.' But if you were to look at the footnote in your Bible you would see it could be translated an 'injurious spirit' and even this was sent by God. In other word it is more akin to a fit of rage—a spirit of temper. This could be no more than a mental condition, a hateful temper which in this context appears to be part of the judgement God sent upon Saul for his rebellion against him and which David could somehow soothe with his harp playing (1 Samuel 16:23).

There is one fleeting reference to demons in Deuteronomy 32:17 in connection with idolatry, such that to worship idols is knowingly or unknowingly to connect with demons.[4]

When we come to the New Testament and the Book of Acts

---

3. The cautionary warning of Peter Bolt should be heeded in this discussion, 'There is a particular danger of falling into unbiblical thinking about evil powers, simply because of the paucity of the biblical evidence. Despite increasingly shrill calls for Christian churches to take evil powers more seriously, it is extremely well recognised that the Bible itself does not really say much about them. The Old Testament is practically silent about demons, then the explosion of references appear as Jesus arrives in the biblical story—at least according to Matthew, Mark and Luke; then there is a tiny demonic dribble into the period of history recorded in Acts, and only an occasional drip elsewhere in the New Testament.' Peter Bolt, 'Defeat of the Evil Powers' in *Christ's Victory Over Evil*, Ed. Peter Bolt (Apollos, 2009), p 39.

4. There are two Hebrew words, both rare in the Old Testament, which are used as generic terms for 'evil spirits'—'demons'—Deuteronomy 32:17; Psalm 106:37 and 'hairy demons' Leviticus 17:7; 2 Chronicles 11:15; Isaiah 13:21; 34:14

there is only *one* case of demon possession and exorcism
related in any detail, that of the fortune-telling slave girl in
Acts 16:16:

> Once when we were going to the place of prayer, we were
> met by a female slave who had a spirit by which she predicted
> the future. She earned a great deal of money for her owners by
> fortune-telling. She followed Paul and the rest of us, shouting,
> 'These men are servants of the Most High God, who are telling
> you the way to be saved.' She kept this up for many days.
> Finally Paul became so annoyed that he turned around and said
> to the spirit, 'In the name of Jesus Christ I command you to
> come out of her!' At that moment the spirit left her.

In the case of Peter in Acts 5:16 we read, 'Crowds gathered
also from the towns around Jerusalem, bringing their sick
and those tormented by evil spirits, and all of them were
healed.' Of Paul in Acts 19 we are told that some evil spirits
left people and folk were cured by taking handkerchiefs
which Paul touched (v 12). Here there seems to be a deliberate
paralleling of Peter as the apostle to the Jews and Paul as
the apostle to the Gentiles. There are in fact a total of five
references in the Book of Acts to evil spirits being cast out.[5]

What is particularly striking is that neither demon
possession nor exorcisms are mentioned in the epistles.
Furthermore, if it is an integral part of ministry, as some
charismatics today would claim, why is it not mentioned in
the pastorals since Timothy and Titus form the bridge from
the apostolic to the post-apostolic age? Although we have
to be careful arguing from silence, in this case the silence is

---

5. 5:15–15; 8:6–7; 16:16–16;19:11–12,13–17

deafening. What is more *no* expulsion of demons by Jesus is recorded in the Gospel of John.[6]

However, *that* the casting out of demons formed an integral part of *Jesus'* ministry is attested to in the synoptic Gospels; Matthew, Mark and Luke.

Jesus and demon possession

Let's think for a moment about Jesus releasing people from demons.[7]

Whilst no casting out of demons is associated with John the Baptist's ministry, once Jesus arrives on the scene, demoniacs appear to be popping up all over the place, that is certainly the impression we get for example in Mark 1:32ff, 'That evening after sunset the people brought to Jesus all the sick and demon-possessed. The whole town gathered at the door, and Jesus healed many who had various diseases. He also drove out many demons, but he would not let the demons speak because they knew who he was.'

---

6. This does not mean of course that there is no consideration of the 'underworld' in John's Gospel. See Willis H. Salier, 'Deliverance without Exorcism?' in *Christ's Victory Over Evil*, ed. Peter Bolt (Apollos, 2009).

7. It might be more accurate to speak of Jesus expelling demons rather than engaging in exorcisms as the latter is associated with ritual, incantations and the like. Whereas with Jesus and the apostles no such ritual occurs which in part might account for the reaction of the people in Mark 1:27. This would also be in line with the Old Testament, 'Whereas in Babylon and Assyria the literature of exorcism plays an important part, there is no trace of these things in the Old Testament, and already at an early date it was forbidden officially to perform any exorcism, sorcery or interrogation of the spirits (Exodus 22:18, 1 Samuel 28; Deuteronomy. 18:9ff; Leviticus 19:31; 20:27).'T. C. Vriezen, *An Outline of Old Testament Theology* (Blackwell, 1958), p. 224

There are six expulsions of demons described in the Synoptics:

1. The demoniac in the synagogue—Mark 1:21/ Luke 4:33

2. Gerasene demoniac/s—Mark 5:1/Matthew 8:28/ Luke 8:26.

3. Daughter of the Syrophoenician woman (Mark 7:24/ Matthew 15:21.

4. The epileptic boy—Mark 9:14/Matthew17:14/Luke 9:37

5. The dumb demoniac—Matthew 9:32.

6. The dumb and blind demoniac—Matthew 12:22.

Of course there were exorcisms being carried out by other Jews long before Jesus came onto the scene since Jesus himself refers to the Pharisees having 'followers' who cast out demons in Luke. 11:19. Jesus' 12 disciples were also given power to cast out demons in Mark 6:13 as were the 72 disciples in Luke 10:17. But it does seem to be the case that there is an unusually *excessive* amount of demonic activity centred on Jesus himself which after his death and resurrection appears to be drastically reduced in comparison.

The question is, why? Why so much activity when Jesus *begins* his ministry and a diminishing when he has finished his earthly ministry?

In Mark's Gospel the casting out of demons underscores the *authority* of Jesus which in turn points to the *divine nature* of Jesus as the Son of God—Mark 1:27, 'The people were all so amazed that they asked each other, "What is this? A new teaching—and with *authority!* He *even* gives orders to impure spirits and they obey him."' It's as if the coming of the Son of God into the world as the world's true King has stirred up a flurry of demonic activity on the part of the prince of this world—the devil—whose rule over people is being threatened. This is quite understandable. Just think about it: it was when the German soil began to be invaded by the Allies during World War 2 that the Nazis fought the most ferociously. This ties in with Jesus' own explanation of the significance of his exorcism in Luke 11: 20 '... if I drive out demons by the finger of God, then *the kingdom of God has come upon you.*' This is a sign that the King has arrived to establish his kingdom. Satan's dominion is being shaken to its very foundations, and the demons know this; Mark 1:24, the demons exclaim, 'What do you want with us, Jesus of Nazareth? Have you come to destroy us? I know who you are—the Holy One of God!' Enemy territory is being reclaimed by its rightful owner and the enemy is stirred to action in desperation.

There are a few more points regarding Jesus and the release of people from the demonic which need to be made.

The first is that Jesus focused not on the devil himself but on the *victims* of the devil's destructive work.

Secondly, while some of Jesus' conflict with Satan was dramatic as in the case of the Gadarene demoniac (Mark 5:1–20), some were less dramatic, as for instance when the devil uses ordinary people with the best intentions to deflect Jesus from carrying out God's purposes. This happened with the apostle Peter in Mark 8. Peter rebuked Jesus for saying that he had to go to the cross with the result that he was rebuked by Jesus with the words, 'Get behind me Satan!' The devil can be at work effectively through the ordinary as well as the extraordinary.

Demon possession and illness

In some cases, demon possession results in a physical ailment such as epilepsy, dumbness or blindness. This has led some to argue that in the case of say, the epileptic boy in Mark 9, this was just ordinary epilepsy and because the organic causes were unknown in Jesus' day it was simply attributed to a demon because they didn't know any better. And so, it is maintained, Jesus was either merely accommodating himself to the ideas of his day or he himself was so locked into the first century world view that he didn't know any different.[8]

This argument is not convincing for a number of reasons.

First, whilst recognising the humanity of Jesus, and so him being subject to human limitations (he couldn't be in two places at once, he grew tired, needed food etc.), in this case he does give a *spiritual* explanation as to the cause of the problem and he carries out an *expulsion* not a *healing*. Contrast this with the case of the woman with some form of spine deformity in Luke 13:10. There we read of this woman having been crippled 'by a spirit' for 18 years. It is not described either as a demon or an unclean/evil spirit. Jesus does not cast it out or address it. He simply put his hands on her and declared her to be set free from her infirmity. So here whilst the term 'spirit' is used, it seems to be used *metaphorically* when we say, for example, we have a 'splitting

---

8. This is linked to what is called the 'kenotic' view of the incarnation, that part of God the Son's emptying of himself (kenosis—Philippians 2:7) was the divesting of certain forms of knowledge.

headache'. But in the case of the epileptic and the other demoniacs, there certainly appears to be a specific personal evil element involved—a demon.

Secondly, unless we have clear evidence to the contrary, to claim that Jesus was simply a 'product of his own time' believing in demons when they don't really exist puts us on a dangerous trajectory. There were notable liberal theologians like Rudolf Bultmann who have argued this position by saying that such language is 'mythological' and merely part of the mental furniture of the first-century world. Some have gone even further and argued that since we don't have to take what Jesus said about heaven and hell, demons and angels literally, then why should we take what he says about prayer and God literally? If one can be jettisoned, why can't the other?[9]

Thirdly, not everyone in the ancient world believed epilepsy was a result of evil spirits. Hippocrates who lived 460 BC argued for organic causes for epilepsy and given the tremendous influence of Greek thought in the Middle East, it is likely that such a view was known by the Jews and certainly to Dr Luke.

Interestingly enough other terms are used to denote mental illness in the New Testament.

1. *Ekstasis*—Mark 3:21; when friends and family came to put Jesus away because they thought him out of his mind,

---

9. The end of this trajectory was reached in the late 1960s with the 'Death of God' school of theology. See T.J. Altizer, *The Gospel of Christian Atheism* (Westminster Press, 1966).

he was 'beside himself'. (It is from this that we get our word 'ecstatic').

2. *Mania*—John 10:20 where the Jews said Jesus was simply 'mad', admittedly, they claimed, as a result of a demon.

3. The term *seleniazomai*—'moonstruck' equivalent to the Latin phrase from which we get our term 'lunatic' is also used in Matthew 4:24 where we read of 'epileptics' as 'moonstricken', translated in the NIV as 'having seizures'. This does not mean that the people at the time believed that such fits were as a result of the waxing and waning of the moon any more than we believe that someone is mentally unstable because of the position of the moon when we call them 'lunatics'. There is a distinction to be made between the origin of a word and its common usage.

It would therefore seem that Jesus and the Bible are well aware of the distinction between a mental illness and a demonic activity, although in some cases they may be connected.

Demon possession and Christians.
If we agree that it is quite understandable there was concentrated demonic activity at the beginning of Jesus' earthly ministry with authoritative exorcisms being signs of Jesus' divine identity; and if it is also a given that signs and wonders were performed as signs of an *apostle* (2 Corinthians 12:12) so we see healings and cleansing from evil spirits occurring in Acts (although they seem to be on the edge of the account with the focus being on proclamation); why do we have *no* instructions about deliverance ministries in the epistles? This question becomes even more acute when we

consider some of the places the apostles ministered such as Ephesus which was *the* occult centre of the ancient world. Surely, deliverance teaching would be expected in Ephesians 6 about Christian warfare if anywhere? But we have nothing of the sort.

Perhaps not quite, 'nothing'! There is a case for arguing that from one standpoint the *whole* letter to the Ephesians gives us some clues as to why things are now different and just *how* Satan wages war on Christians at present.

Here we see that his method of attack is not direct as with demon possession. Furthermore, we discover that the way Christians are to withstand him isn't direct either— 'binding Satan in Jesus' name' and the like. Indeed, there is *no* encouragement given in Scripture for Christians to engage with the devil directly. Certainly we are told by James in his letter to *resist* the devil (4:7) which is not the same thing as *attack* the devil. And even here resisting the devil occurs within the context of renouncing pride by being humble. In other words, one of the principal ways the devil trips Christians up is by appealing to pride, and of course when we become proud that is when we become the most devil-like.

If the truth be told, the situation of the non-Christian is just as serious (maybe more so) than that of the demon possessed in the Gospel accounts, for Ephesians 2:1ff paints the picture of the *whole* human race being under the power of the evil one—'walking according to the ways of this world and the prince of the power of the air.' How is that power broken? By the Word of the Gospel—1:13, 'You were included in Christ when you heard *the word of truth,* the *Gospel* of your salvation'. What is the result? 'We who were dead in trespasses and sins have been made a*live* with Christ', having 'been raised up with him to dwell in the heavenly realms'— heaven where Christ rules (2:6). Something decisive has happened which has broken Satan's grip on the world. That something is the death, resurrection and ascension of the Lord Jesus Christ—the *Gospel*.

Jesus has *all* authority in heaven and earth and *under* the earth (1:2). Therefore, when people come to trust in him, they are raised with Christ and seated with him in the heavenly places (1:1:20–21), this means that in principle they are ultimately out of reach of demonic forces. Christ dwells in them by his Spirit—3:14 and if Christ is in residence then no demon can be. The warfare the Christian wages with the devil is then *external*—battling against false teaching—4:14 and division within the fellowship—4:24.

When faced with these things, in the great chapter on spiritual warfare, Ephesians chapter 6, the Christian is exhorted simply to hold his or her ground—to 'stand'—a command which appears four times. In order to be enabled to do this the Christian has everything he or she needs in the Gospel which is captured by the military image of putting on the whole armour of God. And this, it should be emphasized, is a corporate affair—all of the members of the church doing this and so standing as an army.

There is the helmet of *salvation*, breastplate of *righteousness*, shoes of *peace*, shield of *faith*, belt of *truth*, the sword of God's *Word*—representing different aspects of the Gospel. The one activity Paul does stress, however, is prayer, mentioned three times in verse 18, before going to ask for prayer for himself in order to proclaim the Gospel. Think too of how when the disciples failed to deliver the epileptic boy Jesus said that 'only prayer can drive this kind out'—the implication being that the disciples had tried everything but prayer! In the battle against the underworld prayer is *the* essential element.

It is as the body of Christ, united by faith in him who is our head, with whom we are in heaven, that we share the battle armour as we remain active in the world: 'Therefore, putting on God's armour is an aspect of putting on Christ, that is, being united with Christ through the work of the Holy Spirit, recognizing the riches that he has lavished upon us and responding appropriately by standing firm as a united Church against those dark forces that strive against God's Will.'[10]

Of course, there is also battling the devil in terms of undergoing persecution—1 Peter 5:8 where we are told he appears like a roaring lion which is one of the great themes of the Book of Revelation (especially chapter 12).

The *internal* battle a Christian has however is not with Satan but with *sin*. Contrasting our former way of life under the devil's rule with our new way of life under Christ's rule, Paul writes, 'That, however, is not the way of life you *learned* when you *heard* about Christ and were *taught* in him in accordance with the *truth* that is in Jesus. You were *taught*, with regard to your former way of life, to put off your old self,

---

10. D. R. Reinhard, 'Ephesians 6:10-18: A Call to Personal Piety or Another Way of Describing Union with Christ?', *Journal of the Evangelical Theological Society* 48:521-532 (2005). See also, M. Tinker, 'The Phantom Menace, Territorial Spirits and SLSW', *Churchman* 114:71-81 (2000).

which is being corrupted by its deceitful desires; to be made
new in the attitude of your minds; and to put on the new self,
created to be like God in true righteousness and holiness.'
(Ephesians 4:20ff). Notice that it is all to do with responding
to the *teaching* of the Gospel by which we are changed and
kept free.

The *big* connection made in the Bible is between death and
the devil.

It was through the temptation of Adam and Eve that death
was introduced into the world (Genesis 3/Romans 5), in this
sense the devil has been a 'murderer from the beginning'
according to Jesus in John 8:44, as well as a liar—promising
life while dishing out death. Furthermore, the word 'demon'
was often used in the ancient world to describe the spirits
of the departed with the term 'prince of demons' being
used to describe the being who was the gatekeeper to the
underworld.[11] And so it was seen that the demons used by
magic or necromancy (mediums) were spirits of the dead.
This connection is vital to understand the fuller biblical
picture, because it is by his death on the cross, that Jesus
liberates us from the fear of death and the one who holds
us in its grip, the devil—Hebrews 2:14. 'Since the children
have flesh and blood, he (Jesus) too shared in their humanity
so that by his death he might destroy him who has power
over death—that is the devil' (cf 1 John 3:8). This is the great
deliverance we all need of which the earthly deliverances
performed by Jesus and the apostles were but pointers.

---

11. Ferguson notes that the demons are ghosts in Plutarch, the Greek world and
in the Hellenistic Jews Philo and Josephus—E. Ferguson, *Demonology in the Early
Christian World,* Symposium Series 12 (New York, Edward Mellen).

Sometimes the objection is raised, 'Surely, if a Christian has been involved in occult practices in the past or some relative of his has, might he/she then not have residual demons which need casting out or some occult influence which needs undoing?' Interestingly enough one of the few places where Paul's workings of miracles as a sign of an apostle includes the freeing of people from demons shows this *not* to be the case—Acts 19. Note that here we are not told that Paul engaged in exorcisms, and as far as the miracles were concerned even these were 'extraordinary', and not 'run of the mill' miracles of an apostle—v11. We are told that aprons were touched by Paul to cure folk and release them from demons. This puts them into perspective. In v 18 we have folk who already as believers were confessing their links with the occult and showing repentance by burning the books. This is just another step in the sanctification process amongst many that Christians have to make, a forsaking of things in their past. It would seem that believing the Gospel was enough; no extra special 'deliverance' ministry was needed.

It would seem that as a result of Christ's victory, 'having disarmed the powers and authorities, he made a public spectacle of them, triumphing over them by the *cross*' (Colossians 2:15), a new state of affairs has been introduced into the universe. While Satan and his cohorts are still real, their power has been drastically reduced and as the Kingdom of God advances through the proclamation of the Gospel people are set free.

With a view towards 'the end' as portrayed in Revelation 12, Peter Bolt similarly concludes,

The 'spiritual warfare' in which the Christian is engaged in not a particular aspect of the Christian life, but is the Christian life itself. This explains the need for Christians to be alert and to resist the devil, knowing that he is a defeated enemy and will quickly flee. But there is no call to engage the devil directly, by turning back to the ancient magical practice known as exorcism. Resisting the devil is done through submitting to God (James 4:7). The spiritual warfare of the Christian life is 'fought' by faith, hope and love, through believing the Word of God and praying to our heavenly Father.[12]

Conclusion

Let me end by relating a true story which illustrates the liberating power of the Gospel. It concerns a student I came across when I was chaplain at Keele University, whom we shall call Bill.

Bill wasn't a Christian when I first met him. One day he came to see me in some distress. The reason was that he was having some bad headaches accompanied by dreams which were premonitions of the future. What was really bothering him was that they were all coming true! As we talked it became pretty obvious that he was quite sane. He was a good student, very well-mannered and, as far as one could tell, quite genuine.

The next time we met I asked if, by any chance, he had been involved in any occult practices, such as séances, Ouija boards and the like. He said that although he hadn't directly, his grandmother was a medium and he had been with her in

---

12. Peter Bolt, 'Defeat of Evil Powers', op cit., p. 81

meetings where she tried to contact the dead. I explained to him why this was both wrong and dangerous and that the only sure was to be freed from all of this was to become a Christian. I then explained the Gospel to him and he knew what he had to do in order to commit his life to Christ. Then he went away.

The next time he came to see me he was a different person altogether for he had embraced the Gospel. The premonitions stopped there and then. I continued to disciple him and he grew in Christ. No bell, book or candle stuff, no holy water, just the power of the Gospel prayerfully applied.

7

What is the Church?

Introduction

Several years ago, the evangelical Dutch theologian and writer, Professor Klaas Runia, commented, 'There is an erroneous doctrine of the church, which is so often found among evangelicals. Many of them tend to regard the visible organized Church as relatively unimportant, primarily because in it one finds many who have little faith, if any at all.'

He then went on to urge evangelicals to 'give special attention to the biblical doctrine of the church ... If ever we want to solve the present problems of the church, we must first know what the church really is according to Scripture.'[1]

Since those words were written a good deal of attention has been given to the topic of the church by evangelicals of every stripe.[2] And yet there still appears to be a general haziness

---

1. Klaas Runia, *Reformation Today* (Banner of Truth, 1968) p. 44f.

2. For example, 'The Biblical theology of the Church,' in The Church in the Bible and in the World, ed. D.A. Carson; Tim Bradshaw, *The Olive Branch:*

amongst evangelicals about what the church actually *is*. Some still speak of 'the worldwide church' or the denomination being a 'church', such as the 'Church of England'. But unless such language is checked and qualified by what the *Bible* means when it uses the word, evangelicals are in danger on two fronts. First, being hoodwinked into investing high biblical views of the church into man-made structures such as a denomination with the result that they are held captive by a denominational hierarchy[3] or second, by having such a low regard for the church such that they feel more comfortable in a parachurch setting where matters of doctrine and discipline are not considered to be primary.[4] It is the tendency to move towards one of these two extremes which makes the subject of the church touchy for some people.

However, more positively, to re-capture the Bible's deep view of the church not only invigorates Christian believers as

---

Evangelical Anglican Doctrine of the Church (Latimer Press, 1990); 'Which Church' (Evangelical Press, 2007.)

3. 'Centralized control outside the congregation extinguishes the Gospel within the congregation in due course. History confirms this truth abundantly. Even the smallest degree of control has this effect in the long run, for experience shows that the centre, when given control of the congregation, over the decades increases it, aiming and uniformity and obedience. But the Gospel rocks the boat of the denomination!' D.B. Knox, 'The Church, the Churches and the Denominations of the Churches', reprinted as chapter 5 in *D. Broughton Knox Selected Works: Volume II: Church and Ministry* (Matthias Media, 2003) p 36

4. The dangers of such evangelical movements going astray and the attendant dangers have been well put by Dr Carl Trueman, 'I do believe that parachurch organizations generally suffer from two particular flaws which render them inherently unstable: they are coalition movements, and they typically lack proper structures of accountability.', 'How Parachurch Ministries Go Off The Rails', *The Aquila Report* http://theaquilareport.com/how-parachurch-ministries-go-off-the-rails/ 2011

they seek to make their way through a hostile world as 'aliens and exiles' (1 Peter 2:11), but enables pastors to realize their high calling:

> The church is but the spearhead of a work not merely of urban but also cosmic renewal, an anticipating in its reconciling practices the reconciliation of all things. To confess with the saints across space and through time 'I believe ... in the church' is to confess that the church is the harbinger of the new heavens and the new earth. It is the privilege and responsibility of pastor-theologians to oversee and encourage the church's understanding of and participation in these firstfruits of the new reality 'in Christ.'[5]

The teaching of Jesus

A good place to begin exploring the teaching of the Bible on the church (ecclesiology) is the first time the term 'church' is used by Jesus. This is recorded in Matthew 16:13ff, a passage over which much ink, if not blood, has been spilt in the past!

Verse 13: 'When Jesus came to the region of Caesarea Philippi, he asked his disciples, "Who do people say the Son of Man is?"

They replied, "Some say John the Baptist; others say Elijah; and still others, Jeremiah or one of the prophets." "But what about you?" he asked. "Who do you say I am?" Simon Peter answered, "You are the Messiah, the Son of the living God."'

This passage marks a quantum leap forward in the disciples'

---

5. Kevin J Vanhoozer and Owen Strachan, *The Pastor as Public Theologian: Reclaiming a Lost Vision* (Baker, 2015), p 152

understanding of Jesus, for it is from this point on he begins explicit teaching about his mission which will lead him to the cross (v21ff): 'From that time on Jesus began to explain to his disciples that he must go to Jerusalem and suffer many things at the hands of the elders, chief priests and teachers of the law, and that he must be killed and on the third day be raised to life.' Yes, he is identified as the Messiah. But this is no mere political Christ, hence the cautionary warning of v20: 'he warned his disciples not to tell anyone that he was the Christ.' He was to be a suffering Christ, and so we have an amplification of the Divine Voice heard at Jesus' baptism which links Psalm 2 and Isaiah 42.[6] Peter has now recognized the Psalm 2 part; Jesus teaching in v21ff unpacks the Isaiah part—which is not so readily received—v22: 'Peter took him aside and began to rebuke him. "Never, Lord!" he said. "This shall never happen to you!"' This is the wider setting of which the seminal saying of Jesus in v15ff is a part: '"What about you?" Jesus asked. "Who do you say I am?" Simon Peter answered, "You are the Christ, the Son of the living God." Jesus replied, "Blessed are you, Simon son of Jonah, for this was not revealed to you by man, but by my Father in heaven. And I tell you that you are Peter, and on this rock I will build my church, and the gates of Hades will not overcome it. I will give you the keys of the kingdom of heaven; whatever you bind on earth will be bound in heaven."'

---

6. Psalm 2:7, I will proclaim the Lord's decree: He said to me, 'You are my son; today I have become your father: Ask me, and I will make the nations your inheritance, the ends of the earth your possession. You will break them with a rod of iron, you will dash them to pieces like pottery.'; Isaiah 42:1 'Here is my servant, whom I uphold, my chosen one in whom I delight I will put my Spirit on him, and he will bring justice to the nations'

Two questions immediately spring to mind: What is the church that Jesus is going to build? And what is the 'rock' upon which he is going to build it?

As with many statements of Jesus, the background is the Old Testament and two episodes in particular which relate to God's covenantal promises.[7]

Old Testament Background

The first scene is Mount Sinai.

Here God had called his people to form a gathering to receive the law as he promises that they would be his people and he would be their God. The more immediate background to Jesus' words is Deuteronomy 4:10 where Moses reminds the Israelites of 'the day when you stood before the Lord your God at Horeb when the Lord said to me assemble me a people.' In the Greek translation of the Old Testament (LXX) the word used is *ekklesia* ('church', from which we derive our word 'ecclesiastical') and the verb *ekklesiazo*. An over literal rendering would be, 'the day of the church before the Lord your God at Horeb when the Lord said to me church me a people.' 'Church', then, is a gathering, a crowd, an assembly, a congregation.

Just as *Yahweh* formed his people into a gathering before him at Sinai, having redeemed them from Egypt, which came about by his self-revelation to Moses (Exodus 3), so *Jesus* is going to form *his* church based upon the revelation and

---

7. See D.B Knox, 'De-Mythologising the Church' in Selected Works, Volume 2, Matthias Media, 2003. Also, John Woodhouse, *The Unity that Helps and the Unity that Hinders* (REFORM, 2001) pp. 28–31.

profession of faith given to Peter and the redemption brought about through his sufferings.

The background of Sinai also helps us to understand what Jesus means when he says 'Upon this rock I will build my church—a gathering', which, as we shall see in a moment, is an unfortunate translation.

In Exodus 17:6, the 'rock' before which God's people are to be gathered—'churched'—is Horeb/Sinai, where God is to manifest himself: 'I will stand before you there on the rock of Horeb.' In the Matthew 16 passage Jesus is saying that he is going to form a church in terms drawn from the formation of the Old Testament church of God in the wilderness. Here we may have an implicit claim to deity. As *God* gathered his people before the rock, *Jesus* is gathering his people before 'the rock'. The rock in the Old Testament is Horeb, the location of the LORD before whom the people are gathered. Jesus is similarly going to gather people to himself, who is the rock.

Someone might object, 'Didn't Jesus say "*upon* this rock I will build my church" not "*before* this rock"?' Not necessarily. Early in chapter 7 Matthew used the same words 'build on' 'the rock' in the case of the wise man. But the construction is different. There it is literally 'on top of the rock', but here in Matthew 16 it is 'In front of this rock.' Or 'at the rock.'[8]

Furthermore, the Greek word for 'rock' (*petra*) refers to a solid mass of rock, like a cliff face. Peter (*petros*) means

---

8. In Matthew 7, in dealing with verbs of motion *epi*, 'on', governs the accusative, so the building is 'on top of' the rock. In Matthew 16:18, '*epi*' governs the dative and so it is 'in front of' or 'before' this rock.

a stone, a fragment of a rock mass. As Peter is the first to acknowledge Jesus as 'the rock', by that profession he becomes part of *the* rock—Christ. This is a parallel picture to that of being part of 'the body' or 'the vine'.

The 'rock', then, is not Peter, nor his faith, nor his statement, but Christ.

Let's unpack this a little further.

Peter has in effect declared the Gospel; Jesus is the saving King. This is the message by which people are gathered together in front of their King by the King: it is '*my* church', says Jesus. Furthermore, he is the one who will build it. In this way Peter forms a contrast to Moses in Numbers 20:12: 'The Lord said to Moses and Aaron, because you did not believe in me to sanctify me in the eyes of the children of Israel, you shall not bring them into the Promised Land.' Moses and Aaron share the same fate as all the other unbelievers of the desert church. Peter however had faith, divinely given ('by my Father in heaven'), but nonetheless personal. As a representative of the other disciples, the nascent church which Christ had begun to build with Peter, in a derivative, secondary sense he can be called 'Peter' the 'stone' who is one with 'the Rock.'[9]

The contrast with the fate of Moses and others who died because of unbelief would also explain the reference to Hades or death *not* prevailing against this church (gathering) because of true faith divinely given. Those who belong to

---

9. 'In my view, despite the mixture of metaphors involved, "this rock" refers to Jesus himself, who would then be both the builder and the foundation of the church.' Woodhouse, op cit., p 28

this church will enter *the* ultimate land of promise (Hebrews 4:1–11).

The second Old Testament episode which probably lies behind this saying is the words spoken by Nathan to King David in 2 Samuel 7:12f, in which God declares that he would raise up a son of David and 'I will establish his kingdom. He is the one who will build a house for my name and I will establish the throne of his kingdom forever. I will be his father and he shall be my son.'

Initially this promise points to Solomon whose kingdom will be established (1 Kings 2:46) and the building of the temple in Jerusalem (1 Kings 6). But this kingdom did not last, and so the prophets looked forward to another son of David whose kingdom would be everlasting (Isaiah 9:6–7; 11:1–9; Psalm 2).

In Matthew 16 Peter identifies who that King/Christ is— Jesus of Nazareth. He is the Son of David who will build a house or household for God's name, i.e. he will build his church, gathering a people to himself. The Old Testament temple was the shadow, the type, of which Jesus and his church are the fulfilment and antitype.[10]

If Jesus, the rock, is gathering his people before him—'I will build my church' and we want to know where this church is that Jesus is building, we simply need to ask 'Where is Jesus now?' For where Jesus is, that is where his church will be.

---

10. 'I tell you that something greater than the temple is here' (Matthew 12:6); 'The temple he has spoken of was his body' (John. 2:21); 'I did not see a temple in the city, because the Lord God Almighty and the lamb are its temple' (Revelation 21:22).

The answer is that at present he is in heaven, reigning at the Father's right hand. Therefore, this is the ultimate place to which his people are being gathered.

A Future Fulfilment

This ultimate destiny of the Church (what is often referred to as 'eschatological' fulfilment) is confirmed by the rest of the New Testament. The most obvious book which does so is the Book of Revelation, especially chapter 7:9 and the great multitude that no man can number drawn from every nation and peoples group before the lamb upon his throne. It is also to be seen in Hebrews 12:22ff: 'You have come to mount Zion, the heavenly Jerusalem, the city of the living God, thousands of angels in assembly, the church of the firstborn.' So certain is our salvation (the gates of Hades will not prevail against it—how can they when the church is in heaven?) that in principle Christians can be spoken of as being gathered there *already*—Colossians 3:1-3: 'Since, then, you have been raised with Christ, set your hearts on things above, where Christ is, seated at the right hand of God. Set your minds on things above, not on earthly things. For you died, and your life is now hidden with Christ in God.' This is often referred to by several different terms such as 'the invisible church', 'the universal church', or 'the Catholic church'.[11] This is the church Christ is building as the Gospel is

---

11. The distinction between the 'visible' and 'invisible' church was often made by the Reformers, not to mean that one was more real than the other but as two aspects of the same entity, or in the words of J. I. Packer, 'that which it wears to the eyes of men, who only see the appearance, and that which it has to the eye of God, who looks on the heart and knows things as they are, and whose estimate of spiritual realities, unlike ours, is unerring. J. I. Packer, 'The Doctrine and

proclaimed and believed. What is being claimed, therefore, is that it is the heavenly church is *the goal* of Christ's redeeming work which Jesus goes on to expound in v21ff, a view which is further strengthened by the Sinai/exodus parallel.[12] Ed Clowney writes, 'God's assembly at Sinai is ... the immediate goal of the exodus. God brings his people into his presence that they might hear his voice and worship him. "I am the Lord your God who brought you out of the land of Egypt, out of the land of slavery. You shall have no other gods before me" (Exodus 20:2,3). Standing in the assembly of the Lord, hearing his voice, the people gain their identity from the self-identification of the Lord.'[13] Similarly we gain our identity as the Messiah's people by identifying with the Messiah, gathered before him to hear his voice.

The fact that it is through Gospel proclamation this gathering/church is brought into being is underscored by Matthew 16:19. In contrast to the scribes of Luke 11:52 who because of their approach to the Scriptures 'take away the key of knowledge' and fail to enter the kingdom themselves,

---

Expression of Christian Unity,' in *Serving the People of God: The Collected Shorter Writings of J. I. Packer* (Paternoster,1998) p. 38

12. So John Woodhouse writes, '... this church is the end, the goal of God's purposes, not a means to some other end. Put it another way, the church is what results from the preaching of the Gospel of Jesus Christ in the power of the Spirit, rather than the instrument or agent of the preaching (or some other task). The work of the Gospel is the building of this church. The church does not therefore have a "mission". The common expression "the mission of the church" needs to be rethought. The church is itself the end product of God's mission. The church is not being built in order to carry out some other task-beyond serving before the throne of God day and night' (Revelation 7:15), op cit., pp 31–32

13. 'The Biblical theology of the Church,' in *The Church in the Bible and in the World*, ed. D.A. Carson, p18, Paternoster, 1987.

Peter, by the divine revelation given to him, professes the heart of the Gospel: Jesus as king is the one who ushers in the kingdom. So both in his own right and as a representative of a wider group, Peter can open the kingdom to many as well as shut it. The most striking example of the opening was the day of Pentecost as Peter expounded the Old Testament Scriptures in relation to their fulfilment in Jesus with the result that 3,000 were added to the church that day. An example of a 'binding' is the case of Simon Magus (Acts 8:9–24).

As Jesus' teaching is proclaimed to the end of the age (Matthew 28:18f), disciples are made and the church grows— that is, the heavenly church—and the gates of Hades will not prevail against it.

Where, then does this leave the local churches—the visible church? They are expressions (albeit imperfect expressions) on earth of the heavenly church. Revelation 2–3 affirms this. There we see seven local gatherings and the Risen, ascended Jesus is moving amongst them, his presence mediated by his Spirit. No one church is more or less a church than the others. Each congregation of believers, gathered by the Word of God, is Christ's church. Each one is a visible realization in space and time of the invisible heavenly church which exists in eternity.[14] As we gather as a local church, at the *same time*, we are gathering with the heavenly church.[15]

The Bible asserts that 'Christ loved the church, and gave himself up for her' (Ephesians 5:25). The context of Ephesians strongly suggests that Paul has both the universal church and the local church in mind—or, better put, the assembly of the local church is a kind of outcropping in history of the assembly of the church of the living God already gathered in solemn assembly before the throne in union with Christ. This is true of several passages that presuppose a porous interface between the universal church and the local church. For example, in Matthew 16, Jesus says, 'I will build my church, and the gates of Hades will not overcome it,' while two chapters later disputants

---

14. Similarly, writing in 1950, Alan Stibbs argues, 'To sum up the two sides of our Lord's teaching about the church, we may say, on the one hand, that the one great church of God exists invisibly in the heavenly places. It is to Christians an object of faith, not of sight. On the other hand, the only thing that exists visibly in the world as an earthly counterpart to this heavenly fellowship is the local churches, the meeting together in many places of those who profess the faith of Christ ... It is, therefore, surely of some significance that the New Testament writers never use the word 'church' in the singular to suggest one great visible earthly organization. In contrast to any such idea, the Apostle Paul speaks deliberately and in some ways very surprisingly in the plural of 'the churches' ... There is, therefore, no scriptural ground for looking for the emergence of one ecumenical or worldwide church as a visible earthly organization, having, like an earthly empire, a geographical centre and a human head.' A. M. Stibbs, 'The New Testament Teaching Concerning the Church', reprinted in *Such a Great Salvation: Collected Essays of Alan Stibbs*, edited by A. Atherstone (Mentor, 2008), pp 231–235

15. A similar thought is captured by Vanhoozer and Strachan when they write, 'The church, then, is no ordinary building. It is rather a heavenly temple, a place where God's will is being done on earth as it is in heaven. The church, the people joined together in Christ, is the place where God's life, light, and love becomes lived out in space and time', op cit., p151

are to tell it to the church, which can scarcely be the universal church. The local church is the historical manifestation, under the new covenant, of this massive, blood-bought assembly.[16]

What's in a name?

It is within the context of the above Biblical framework of Jesus' teaching, Old Testament hopes and eschatological fulfilment, the actual word 'church'—*ekklesia*—finds its natural meaning. Elsewhere the word's primary meaning is gathering which does not always have a religious association—e.g. Acts 19:32: 'The assembly (*ekklesia*) was in confusion', referring to a pagan mob! But as we have seen, what is an ordinary word to describe a gathering is given special significance when applied to God's act of gathering a covenant people.

Generally, *ekklesia* is the Greek rendering of the Hebrew *qahal*. It is a term which describes the covenant making assembly at Sinai (Deuteronomy 9:10) as well as Israel gathered before God for covenant renewal (Deuteronomy 29:1). This view is confirmed by Stephen in Acts 7 where he uses the word 'church' to describe the Old Testament congregation of God. In the New Testament it is a term almost exclusively applied to Christian *communities* after Pentecost.

In the epistles, it is significant that the plural is used when more than one church is in view: 'The *churches* of God' (2 Thessalonians 1:4) and the '*churches* of God in Judea'

---

16. D. A. Carson, 'Why the Local Church Is More Important Than TGC, White Horse Inn, 9Marks, and Maybe Even ETS', *Themelios* 40.1 (2015): 1–9

(2 Thessalonians 2:14, cf.1 Corinthians 7:17; Romans 16:4; Galatians 1:2). There are a few exceptions to the plural form. Paul speaks of 'every church' in 1 Corinthians 4:17—a distributive expression, or 'the church of God' 1 Corinthians 10:32, used in a generic or localized sense.[17] Otherwise, it is a term which is only applied to *an actual gathering of people*. There are, however, a few instances of an extension of the literal, descriptive use of *ekklesia* to denote persons who compose that gathering whether present or not: Acts 8:3; 9:31; 20:17.[18]

If the emphasis is upon 'gathering' by Christ through the Gospel, then 'church' is more of an *event* than an entity. This was a point made by Donald Robinson over 50 years ago, '"Church" is not a synonym for "people of God"; it is rather an activity of the "people of God". Images such as "aliens and exiles" (1 Peter 2:11) apply to the people of God in the world, but do not describe the church, i.e. the people assembled with Christ in the midst (Matthew 18:20; Hebrews 2:12).'[19]

---

17. P. T. O'Brien has provided a comprehensive and detailed biblical treatment of this understanding of the relation between church—local and Church—universal or heavenly. He summarises the Pauline usage as follows, 'Paul consistently refers to the church which meets in a particular place. Even when there are several gatherings in a single city (e.g., Corinth) the individual assemblies are not understood as part of the church in that place, but as one of the churches that meet there. This suggests that each of the various local churches are manifestations of that heavenly church, tangible expressions in time and space of what is heavenly and eternal.' P. T. O'Brien, *Colossians and Philemon, Word Commentary Series* (Word 1982), p 61

18. The few exceptions to the rule ... are all references to the Jerusalem church, 'throughout the first generation it was *"the church par excellence"* (so Acts 9:31; 18:22; 1 Cor. 15:9; Gal. 1:13; Phil. 3:6). See how Paul impressed this perspective on his churches in Rom. 15:27.' Woodhouse, op. cit., 33

19. Robinson, 'Church', *New Bible Dictionary*, ed. JD Douglas (IVP, London, 1962), reprinted as chapter 18 in *Donald Robinson: Selected Works Volume 1*,

Holding together Local and Universal church

How, then, might the universal and local church be seen to be related?

Perhaps the universal church can be construed along the lines of thought expressed in Hebrews 12:22–24.

> But you have come to Mount Zion, to the heavenly Jerusalem, the city of the living God. You have come to thousands upon thousands of angels in joyful assembly, to the church of the first born, whose names are written in heaven. You have come to God, the judge of all men, to the covenant, and to the sprinkled blood that speaks a better word than the blood of Abel.

The implication is that Christians participate in the heavenly church of Jesus Christ both on the basis of being united to him by faith and by gathering with fellow believers where Christ is present by his Spirit.[20] Each *congregation* is the full expression, in that place, of the one true heavenly church. Or to use Paul's favoured expression, 'the Body of Christ', it is not that each local congregation is to be seen as one member parallel to lots of other members which together make up Christ's body—the church. Nor is each church the body of Christ, as if Christ has many bodies. Rather, each

---

Assembling God's People (Australian Church Record 2007) p 223

20. 'This gathering is both heavenly and eschatological. Christians in their conversion have already, in a sense, come to God and reached Mount Zion, the heavenly Jerusalem, the city of the living God. At the same time, the city to come is still the goal of their pilgrimage (13:14; 4:1–11). Hebrews reflects the 'already/not yet' tension found elsewhere in the New Testament. Here in12:22–24 the 'already' pole of that tension is accented.' Peter T O'Brien, *The Letter to the Hebrews, Pillar New Testament Commentary* (Apollos, 2010) p 491

church is an outcrop or colony of heaven, reflecting the heavenly gathering of God's people around the heavenly throne.[21]

Let's explore and tease out the implications of this a little further as laid down in Hebrews chapters 12 and 13.

First, a contrasting parallel is being drawn between the way God gathered his people around himself at Sinai (v18 c.f. Exodus 19:4, 5) and Christ gathering his people around himself; vv23-24. These Christians gathered are the church of the firstborn (cf. Exodus 13:2) approaching God through Christ the mediator, on the basis of a new covenant established by his blood. This is a present reality: 'You have come (present tense—*proseleluthate*) to Mount Zion and to the city of the living God ...' When Christians gather on earth they *at the same time* gather around Christ's throne in heaven.

It is in the midst of the heavenly church that Christ is now seated (Revelation 7:9; 14:1). In principle Christians are already seated there with him (Ephesians 2:6). It is this heavenly church that Christ is building and against which the gates of Hades will not prevail (Matthew 16:18).

Furthermore, the heavenly church is to be equated with the 'universal' church and the 'catholic' church of the Nicene Creed, 'I *believe* in one holy, catholic and apostolic church'. It is an object of faith precisely because it cannot be seen. It is also the principle of unity that by definition there can only be

---

21. To see how this view ties in with that of the Magisterial Reformers see, Peter Sanlon and Melvin Tinker, 'The Ecclesiastical Posture of an Evangelical', *Churchman* 123/4, 2009

one gathering in heaven around the throne of the lamb. It is universal in that it is composed of people 'from every nation, tribe and language' (Revelation 7:9).[22]

To sum up: what is spoken of as the universal or Catholic church is the heavenly church. It is a present eschatological reality gathered round the risen ascended Christ. All true believers belong to this gathering and are members of it. As Christians gather on earth—as the local church—they at the same time reflect something of the heavenly gathering, as well as participate in it.[23]

Being Church

How is the local church brought into being and what is to characterise it?

The gathering is realised by the Word of the Gospel, and so

---

22. 'It is logically impossible for him to assemble two churches around himself, for Christ is to be thought of as one place only, that is, in heaven, if we were to use biblical imagery, which is the only imagery available. This gathering or church is holy, because it is God's ... It is catholic because the Gospel is no longer confined to the literal seed of Abraham, but rather Christ is gathering into his church "out of every nation and of all tribes and peoples and tongues". It is apostolic because it is founded on the apostles, that is to say, Christ commissioned missionaries who founded the church by preaching the Gospel of Christ. It is the heavenly church which is apostolic (Revelation 21:14) as well as catholic, holy and indivisibly one.' D. B. Knox, 'The Church' and 'The Denominations', *Sent by Jesus* (Banner of Truth 1992), p 57

23. 'Every Christian gathering may be regarded as an earthly expression of the heavenly church. Even now the members of the Messiah's community find the reality of God in their midst, in their holy fellowship. But this is only an anticipation of the ultimate reality, the fellowship of the heavenly city or the "new Jerusalem", which will one day come down "out of heaven from God"' (Revelation 21:1-4), D. G. Peterson, *Engaging with God: A Biblical Theology of Worship* (Apollos, 1992), p 205

the proclamation of that Word is to be the central activity and one of the defining features of the gathering.

When God gathered his people at Sinai we read: 'The Lord *spoke* to you out of the midst of the fire, you heard the sound of words, but saw no form.' (Deuteronomy 4:9) This constitutes the contrasting parallel with what happens when Christians gather according to Hebrews 12:18ff: 'You have *not* come to a mountain ... or to such a *voice* speaking words that those who heard it begged that no further word be spoken.' As New Testament believers gather, they come to 'God the judge of all men'. How is such a 'coming to God' made possible? It is through 'Jesus the mediator of a new covenant, and the sprinkled blood that speaks a better *word* than the blood of Abel.' It is this word which gathers people into Christ's body. As it is believed people are incorporated into him. It was the great Pentecostal gift (Acts 2) which led to 3,000 being added to that assembly in a single day.

What is more, it is this word of grace (Acts 20:32) which nourishes the spiritual health of the church. This is why the writer of Hebrews goes on in v25 to say, 'See to it that you do not refuse him who speaks' [which is what the Sinai 'church' did—they did not wish to hear that voice]. How does one hear this voice? Earlier in the letter we are told: 'So, as the Holy Spirit *says* [present tense]' and thereafter follows a quotation from Scripture (Psalm 95) "Today, if you hear his voice do not harden your hearts."' It is through the Scriptures that God the Holy Spirit speaks. The same Word that he spoke *then* is the same Word he speaks *now*.

For this purpose of building up the church God has appointed leaders, which is why the writer exhorts,

'Remember your leaders, who spoke the word of God to you. Consider the outcome of their way of life and imitate their faith ... Do not be carried away by all kinds of strange teachings.' (13:7–9) Further, 'Obey your leaders and submit to their authority. They keep watch over your souls as men who must give an account.' (13:17)

Holiness is to be a mark of the church: 'Make every effort to live in peace with all men and to be holy, without holiness no-one will see the Lord.' (12:14) This is linked to the call to brotherly love: 'Keep loving each other as brothers. Do not forget to entertain strangers ... remember those in prison as if you were their fellow prisoners.' (13:1–3) 'And do not forget to do good and to share with others, for with such sacrifices God is pleased' (13:16).

One aspect of the church which reflects the heavenly assembly is praise: 'You have come to angels in joyful assembly.' (12:22) 'Through Jesus, therefore let us continually offer to God a sacrifice of praise—the fruit of lips that confess his name.' (13:15). Another notable activity which should characterise the earthly gathering is prayer: 'Pray for us ... I particularly urge you to pray so that I may be restored to you soon.' (13:20). 'The saints gather together as a local church to be built up on faith, hope, and love for the ultimate purpose of becoming the kind of people who can worship in spirit and truth anywhere and anytime.'[24]

All these things are being achieved in the church by its great pastor who gathers them to form his 'little flock' and who is in their midst by his Spirit: 'May the God of peace, who

---

24. Vanhoozer and Strachan, op. cit., p 168

through the blood of the eternal covenant brought back from the dead our Lord Jesus, that great Shepherd of the sheep, equip you with everything good for doing his will, and may he work in us what is pleasing to him, through Jesus Christ.' (13:20).

Conclusion

A number of years ago the Bible translator, J. B. Phillips, published a book entitled *Your God is too small* to challenge the Christian's often diminished view of the God of Scripture. We may similarly be challenged about our view of the church as being 'too small'. Instead of being content with overbearing denominationalism on the one hand or a diminished congregationalism on the other, the picture the Bible presents of God's great activity of gathering through the proclamation of the Gospel of the Lord Jesus Christ is simply breathtaking. The scene of the great 'church' in Revelation 7 and its great song of salvation, provides the eternal backdrop for what takes place when even 'two or three' are gathered in Jesus' name (Matthew 18:15–20):

> After this I looked, and there before me was a great multitude that no one could count, from every nation, tribe, people and language, standing before the throne and before the Lamb. They were wearing white robes and were holding palm branches in their hands. And they cried out in a loud voice: 'Salvation belongs to our God, who sits on the throne, and to the Lamb.'

It is as we focus our attention on this great spiritual reality and its local expression in the congregation that Christ will be honoured and hearts will be stirred to worship and service.

8

Are Science and Christianity enemies or friends?

Introduction

During the latter half of the 19th century and the early 20th century, the view began to be popularized that science and religion (more specifically Christianity), were fundamentally at odds with each other. The metaphor which became dominant to describe the relationship was that of 'warfare'. Books began to appear which generated what has become known as the 'conflict thesis' with such titles as *A History of the Conflict between Religion and Science* (J. W. Draper, 1875); *A History of the Warfare of Science with Theology in Christendom* (A. D. White, 1896); and *Landmarks in the Struggle between Science and Religion* (J. Y. Simpson, 1925).[1] Such a view that Christianity and science are to be seen as enemies rather than friends continues to be propagated by

---

1. See, 'The Warfare Merchants', in Denis Alexander, *Rebuilding the Matrix: Science and Faith in the 21st Century* (Lion, 2001), pp 177–219

Professor Richard Dawkins amongst others. However, I hope to demonstrate that such an alleged conflict is more apparent than real and is, to use a term of Professor Keith Ward, a 'Phantom Battle'.[2] I want to show this by arguing that if Christianity and Science were fundamentally opposed to each other then three things would necessarily follow: 1. Science and Christianity would contradict each other. 2. From the very beginning science would have had no truck with Christianity and 3. As science has progressed fewer scientists would be religious.

Do science and Christianity contradict each other?

In order to answer this question, consider the following parable:

Dr Pedant of Secular University is a physicist by training and is so absorbed in his subject that everything has to be seen through the lens of his beloved 'hard' science. To be frank, this makes Dr Pedant something of a nerd. How so? Let me illustrate how by relating what happened to him one day. He received through the post a rather affectionate letter written by a young lady who had admired Dr Pedant from afar. Her heart had been captured by the young scientist. How handsome he looked in his white laboratory coat. His horn-rimmed glasses sent her into a swoon. The high forehead was obviously a sign of superintelligence, and she liked that in a man. All these things she set forth in her epistle, wearing her heart on her sleeve in the hope that Dr Pedant might feel the same way about her.

---

2. Keith Ward, *The Turn of the Tide—Christian belief in Britain Today* (BBC Publications, 1986), Chapter 2.

You had to hand it to Ethel: she was not backward in coming forward!

How did Dr Pedant respond? He responded as any scientist of his ilk would. He became excited when he opened the letter and noticed the quality of the paper which had been used. He took it along to the laboratory to examine its cellulose and water content. Yes, he was right, this was a most interesting chemical composition indeed: he might write an article on it for the next issue of Scientists' Weekly. Then there was the ink. He subjected it to chromatographic analysis, separating out the different pigments which composed it. The results were fed into a computer, which produced some very interesting figures.

But later on that day a friend said to Dr Pedant, 'I see you received a letter today: who was it from and what did it say?' Being the hard-nosed scientist he was, of the old 'positivist' school, he replied, 'Don't ask me, I am a scientist. Take it to the linguistics department if you want to ask those sorts of questions. As far as I am concerned they are just random marks on a page.'[3]

Our apocryphal scientist is obviously an extreme case, but he does help make the valid point that in a similar way modern-day scientists can offer their views about the origin of the universe, the beginnings of humankind, and the biological nature of human beings by analyzing such things in scientific terms, using scientific methods, and still not be able to answer the most vital questions of all, which are to do with the meaning and purpose of humankind: Who are we?

3. See Melvin Tinker, *Reclaiming Genesis* (Monarch, 2010), pp 38–40

Why are we here? Where are we going? How are we meant to behave? Is there a mind behind this universe? However, when scientists *do* attempt to answer such questions they can no more give an answer *as scientists* than Dr Pedant could, with the result that they miss out on the most important thing: in his case, that someone was trying to establish a relationship. If they do speak about such things—as the famous Professor Dawkins has done at length—they are going *beyond* science and their views are not necessarily any better or worse than anyone else's.

Put boldly and simply, science is the language of the 'what' and 'how' (cf the material composition of the letter) and Christianity is the language of the 'why' or 'meaning' (cf the content and intent of the letter).

What is science?

Science involves a specialised method and approach which, in a highly organised way, seeks to explain natural phenomena and those explanations are always subject to modification through further observations. This means that science has two parts: *theory and research.*[4] The theory is made up of abstract statements about why and how some portion of nature fits together and works. From these scientists are able to make predictions about what should and shouldn't be observed. This is where research comes in, for it makes those observations that are relevant to the testable predictions.

This flags up a very important point to remember, namely,

---

4. See Rodney Stark, 'God's Handiwork', in *For the Glory of God* (Princeton University Press, 2002), p 124

science has *limits* both in terms of its methods and concepts. Scientists are concerned with the *physical* world of matter and energy and mechanisms—the 'how?' questions—e.g. 'How is the letter composed in terms of its material elements?' This means that some things lie outside the realm of science, not least the question of the existence and nature of God. As the distinguished biologist, Francisco J. Ayala has said, 'The scientific view of the world is hopelessly incomplete,' and there are 'matters of value, meaning and purpose that are outside science's scope'.[5]

If God is the supreme being who exists *outside* space and time and yet maintains space and time 'by the Word of his power' (Hebrews 1:3), then to claim there can't be a God because science cannot find him in the universe is like someone claiming that Shakespeare couldn't exist because he can't be identified by a literary critic to be anywhere in the 'Denmark' of the play *Hamlet*. God is the author of the *whole* show, in a similar way to Shakespeare being the author of *Hamlet*. How we find out about God will involve other questions and methods which are *beyond* science. The Chief Rabbi, Jonathan Sacks describes the essential difference between the two enterprises in this way: 'Science takes things apart to see how they work. Religion puts things together to see what they mean.'[6]

---

5. F.J. Ayala, quoted by Alister McGrath 'A Fine Tuned Universe', The 2009 Gifford Lectures, Lecture 6, p. 18, www.abdn.ac.uk/gifford

6. Jonathan Sacks, *The Great Partnership: God, Science and the Search for Meaning* (Hodder, 2011), p.55. He elucidates the difference in this way, 'Science is the search for explanation. Religion is the search for meaning. Meaning is not accidental to the human condition because we are the meaning-seeking animal.

Please don't think that I am saying that as far as science is concerned it is a matter of 'Hands off God and religion'[7] as if Christians and theologians were claiming proprietorial rights! It is a matter of ensuring that we recognise that science, while incredibly fruitful in its own sphere, has methodological and conceptual limitations—it's not a matter of territory but method.

Let's go back to our parable.

If science deals effectively with the 'how' questions ('how is the letter constituted'), there are other questions which it not only doesn't answer but cannot answer in principle—namely, the 'why' questions (matters of meaning and purpose), such as 'It is a love letter.' Questions of value, morality and purpose lie outside the realm of science. This is common sense. Indeed, this was something recognised by one no less than Albert Einstein:

> For science can only ascertain what is, but not what should be, and outside of its domain value judgements of all kinds remain necessary ... representatives of science have often made an attempt to arrive at fundamental judgements with respect to values and ends on the basis of scientific method, and in

---

To believe on the basis of science that the universe has no meaning is to confuse two disciplines of thought: explanation and interpretation.' p 37

7. 'I think we are justified in speaking of the 'limits of science' only in a *methodological* rather than *territorial* sense. Designed for situations—all situations—from which an observer can remain detached, certain aspects of the scientific approach automatically ceases to apply when detachment is impossible.' Donald M. MacKay, *The Clockwork Image* (Inter Varsity Press, 1974), p 38

this way have set themselves in opposition to religion. These conflicts have all sprung from fatal errors.[8]

However, there are more basic questions the Bible seeks to answer—the 'why' questions: 'Why is there a universe at all and what is our place in it? How are we meant to relate to God, to each other and to the world?'

In answer to these questions the Bible claims that there is an infinite-personal God who has brought this universe into being (and, many would argue, leaves open the question as to 'how' he has done that).[9] What is more, he sustains it, by the 'word of his power' according to the writer to the Hebrews (1:3). This means that if God were to withdraw that sustaining power, there wouldn't be, as is often imagined, chaos, with planets and stars colliding into each other—there would be *nothing*.

The basic claim that God is Creator of all that exists is found in the opening words of Genesis 1, 'In the Beginning God created the heavens and the earth'. That God is the sustainer and provider of everything is the great theme of Psalm 104, v10:

> He (God) makes springs pour water into the ravines; it flows between the mountains. They give water to all the beasts of the field; the wild donkeys quench their thirst. The birds of the air nest by the waters; they sing among the branches. He waters the mountains from his upper chambers; the earth is satisfied

---

8. Albert Einstein, *Out of My Later Years* (New York Philosophical Library, 1950), p 25

9. See Melvin Tinker, 'Clearing Away Conceptual Fog: Genesis, Creation and Evolution', *Churchman*, Vol 126/ 2 (2012), pp.103–114.

by the fruit of his work. He makes grass grow for the cattle, and plants for man to cultivate—bringing forth food from the earth: wine that gladdens the heart of man, oil to make his face shine, and bread that sustains his heart.

Of course scientific descriptions of all of these things can be offered in terms of the categories of meteorology and biology, using scientific language such as 'photosynthesis', 'enzyme production' and the like, but that would not rule out the deeper *theological* explanation given using poetic language as we have it in the psalm. Therefore, we can and should pray, 'Give us our daily bread' for as the Psalmist goes on to write: 'These all look to you to give them their food at the proper time. When you give it to them, they gather it up; when you open your hand, they are satisfied with good.' Such a prayer does not mean that we somehow deny scientific explanations of wheat production and bread making; rather it is an expression of the acknowledgement that the ultimate source of all such gifts is a personal God who far from being removed from his creation (as in Deism) is intimately involved in every aspect of it.

From a Christian point of view modern science is the proper means and method of exploring and understanding God's creation. No more and no less. Or, in the words of the first person to produce the first accurate working model of the solar system—Johannes Kepler—science is a matter of 'thinking God's thoughts after him.' Within this framework of understanding, science and Christianity are therefore not *contradictory* but *complementary*. This was the standpoint of many early 19th century thinkers. It is not widely known that the term 'scientist' was actually coined by a 19th century ordained Church of England minister, William Whewell. Before that they were called 'natural philosophers'. Whewell was a double professor at Cambridge University occupying one chair in mineralogy and another in moral philosophy. He also coined many other terms which are now part of our language such as 'physicist', 'anode', and 'cathode'. He saw no conflict of substance between what the Bible taught and what science taught because there isn't one.

Have science and Christianity been enemies from the beginning?

If there is an intrinsic battle between science and Christianity as some allege, then it would be reasonable to assume that at least such tensions would have existed from the very beginning of the modern scientific enterprise. The evidence points in the opposite direction, that Christianity *gave rise* to modern science.

First of all it is necessary to go back a little and take a brief look at the contrast between pagan views of nature and the biblical view in order to see how it was this biblical outlook which not only provided the rational grounding upon which modern science could develop (as well as much of its motivation) but also positively laid upon people the obligation to engage in this enterprise, it being seen as part of the creation mandate to 'fill the earth and subdue it' (Genesis 1:28). Given that 'contrast is the mother of clarity' a comparison between the two views will show that at root there is no final conflict between science and the Christian faith.

The contrast between Greek views of nature and that of

the Bible, together with the seminal influence of biblical Christianity on the development of modern science, has been well documented by Professor R Hooykaas.[10]

He summarizes the Greek understanding of nature, going back through the Stoics, Aristotle, Plato and the Eleatic philosophers of the fifth century, under four points:

The Greeks did not admit creation; to them nature herself was eternal and uncreated. Nature worship was never totally removed from Greek thought, although it developed into a highly intellectualized form. Therefore it was simply 'not on' to pry too closely into her secrets—the legend of Prometheus captures the Greek understanding well. What is more, it was held that it was impossible to do anything against nature. Even for Plato in his *Timaeus*, the 'Demiurge' who shaped the world according to a definite plan had his hands tied in two important respects. First, he had to follow the model of eternal ideas, and secondly he had to put the stamp upon recalcitrant matter which he had not created.

The Greek conception of nature was not only rational, it was *rationalistic*. To the Greeks what was not rational was not real, and only what was real (that is, not subject to change) could be known. In nature logical necessity reigned. Therefore, mathematics with its ideal and unchangeable objects was the type of true knowledge. Astronomy was slightly inferior and the terrestrial sciences, where there is so much change, were hardly worth bothering with at all.

---

10. R. Hooykaas, *Religion and the Rise of Modern Science* (Eerdmans, 1974.) Also, Hooykaas, *The Christian Approach in Teaching Science* (Tyndale Press, 1966).

The disregard of matter led the Greek idealistic philosophers to undervalue observation and experiment. Plato, for example, mocked the Pythagoreans for their 'torturing instruments' in order to obtain knowledge.

The disregard of manual labour led not only to the undervaluing of experimentation but also to that of applied science. Aristotle was of the opinion that all useful things had already been invented.

The contrast with the biblical view could not be greater.

First of all, the Bible spells freedom from any tyranny to 'nature', for even this is put under the dominion of man (cf. Psalm 8); so that in principle there is no aspect of creation which is a scientific 'no go' area. Experiment, technology and even art does not have to copy nature: they can actually go against it without any fear of reprisal (*hubris*).

According to the biblical account, God created according to his own sovereign free will so that one cannot say beforehand that certain things are impossible, he is not bound by what we would claim to be 'objective reason'. God has established rules in his creation, and it is by humble investigation that we are to discover the extent to which they are conformable to our reason.

What God has created he pronounced 'good' (fit for purpose), so that the study of material nature is a religious duty; matter is not to be looked down upon. Furthermore, manual labour is not some inferior activity: God instituted it (in Genesis 2 Adam is portrayed as a gardener to 'care' for the garden in priestly terms)[11], and he himself did not shrink from becoming a carpenter.

Hooykaas puts the contrast as follows:

> The Bible knows nothing of 'Nature' but only knows of 'creatures' who are absolutely dependent upon their origin and existence upon the will of God. Consequently, the natural world is admired as God's work and as evidence of its Creator, but is never adored. Nature can arouse in man a feeling of awe but this is conquered by the knowledge that man is God's fellow worker who shares with him the rule of the fellow creatures, the 'dominion over the fish of the sea and the fowl of the air ...' Thus, in total contrast to Pagan religion, nature is not a deity to be feared and worshipped, but a work of God to be admired, studied and managed. In the Bible, God and nature are no longer both opposed to man, but God and man together confront nature.[12]

It is not possible to over-emphasize the radical and liberating effect of this biblical outlook. It results in science being an activity which is actually pleasing to God. Obedience to the truth—what you find by observation and experiment—becomes central, so that one is no longer bound by preconceived ideas of what can or cannot be the case: to put it crudely, if you want to know what a thing is like—go and look! Indeed, science could be seen as part of Christian charity, a duty whereby the findings of science could be used to benefit one's fellow human beings. We see, for instance, in

---

11. See Melvin Tinker, 'Clearing Away Conceptual Fog', p 111 (*Churchman* 126/2, 2012)

12. Hooykaas, *Religion and the Rise of Modern Science*, p 8.

the works of Francis Bacon the ideal of science being used in man's service, and so he concludes his preface to his *Historia Naturalis* with the prayer: 'May God, the Founder, Preserver and Renewer of the Universe, in His love and compassion to men, protect the work both in its ascent to his glory and its descent to the good of Man, through His only Son, God-with-us.'

Certainly, as Bacon himself stressed, such activity was to be done in a spirit of humility—humility before God and the creation as he has made it. And so in 1605 in his *Advancement of Learning*, he spoke of God giving us two books to read, the Book of God's Word—the Bible and the book of God's Works—nature. Both, he said, are to be studied with diligence as both are given by God.[13] Also, as

---

13. Bacon chose as his title for his principal scientific work *Novum Organum* to replace a medieval compilation of the works of Aristotle, the *Organon*. He saw that such philosophy put unbiblical constraints in seeking out knowledge, 'many have not only considered it to be impossible but also as something impious to try to efface the bounds nature seem to put to her works', but he argued it was 'heathen arrogance, not the Holy Scripture, which endowed the skies with the prerogative of being incorruptible'. In fact he went even further to argue that Aristotle's philosophy made not only science but also faith in God impossible, 'When he [Aristotle] had made nature pregnant with final causes, laying it down that "Nature does nothing in vain, and always affects her will when free from impediments", and many other things of the same kind [he] had no further need of God'—cited by Denis Alexander in *Rebuilding the Matrix* (Lion, 2001), p. 86. A case has been made that it was an undermining of Aristotelian metaphysics that lay at the root of the conflict between the Church of Rome and Galileo. Pietro Rendondi has discovered documentary evidence that the charge of Copernicanism levelled at Galileo was really a cover-up for an even more serious charge of heresy concerning the Mass. According to Rendondi, Galileo's theory of atoms undermined the doctrine of transubstantiation; see Pietro Rendondi, *Galileo Heretic* (Princeton University Press, 1987).

we see in Newton, the founders of the Royal Society and the Puritans, men like John Wilkins (Oliver Cromwell's brother-in-law), whatever is done is to the 'glory of God'. And so it was within the milieu of Protestant Christianity in particular that modern science was launched.

Here is the assessment of one leading historian of science, Stanley Jaki:

> The scientific quest found fertile soil only when faith in a personal, rational Creator had truly permeated a whole culture, beginning with the centuries of the High Middle Ages. It was that faith which provided, in sufficient measure, confidence in the rationality of the universe, trust in progress, and an appreciation of the qualitative method, all indispensable ingredients of the scientific quest.[14]

In 1925 in his Lowell lectures, the non-Christian and co-author with the atheist Bertrand Russell of *Principia Mathematica* (1910–1913), A.N. Whitehead made the same point. He argued that you had to have a sufficient basis for *believing* that the scientific enterprise would be worthwhile and Christianity supplied it. He pointed out that the images of gods found in other religions, especially Asia, are too impersonal or too irrational to have sustained science. Obviously, if you believed that there were gods who are fickle and keep changing their minds, you could never engage in science, because that is dependent upon things being stable and not being changed on a whim. The God of the Bible provides such stability. Christianity is the root, and science the fruit.

---

14. Stanley L. Jaki, *Science and Creation* (University Press of America, 1990).

Here is Professor Rodney Stark making the same point:

> The rise of science was not an extension of classical learning. It was the natural outgrowth of Christian doctrine. Nature exists because it was created by God. To love and honour God, one must fully appreciate the wonders of his handiwork. Moreover, because God is perfect, his handiwork functions in accord with immutable principles. By the full use of our God-given powers of reason and observation, we ought to be able to discover these principles.[15]

But what stance does a Christian take when there appears to be a conflict between 'the Book of nature' and the 'Book of Scripture'? A helpful and cautionary principle has been laid down by the later Professor Donald M. Mackay,

> It is impossible for a scientific discovery given by God to contradict a Word given by God. If therefore a scientific discovery, as distinct from scientific speculation, contradicts what we have believed by the Bible, it is not a question of error in God's Word, but of error in our way of interpreting it. Far from 'defending' the Bible against scientific discovery, the Christian has a duty to welcome thankfully, as from the same Giver, whatever light each may throw upon the other. This is the 'freedom' of a fully Christian devotion to the God of Truth.[16]

---

15. Rodney Stark, *For the Glory of God* (Princeton University Press, 2003), p. 157.

16. D.M. Mackay, 'Science and the Bible,' in *The Open Mind and other essays*, ed. Melvin Tinker (IVP, 1988) p 150.

Do we have less religious scientists than in the past?

If the science versus religion thesis is correct then one might expect that with the passage of time and the development of science there would be significantly *less* professional scientists who would be religious.[17]

This is not the case.

In 1914 the American psychologist, James Leuba, sent questionnaires to a random sample of people listed in American Men of Science—the top scientists of his day. He hoped to show that scientific thinking people would *not* be very religious and that in due course society as a whole would grow out of such superstitious beliefs. Each was asked to select one of the following statements: 1. I believe in a God to whom one may pray in the expectation of receiving an answer. 2. I do not believe in God as defined above. 3. I have no definite belief regarding this question. This is so stringent it would exclude some modern clergy! To his dismay Leuba found that 41.8% of these prominent scientists selected option one. 41.5% (many whom Leuba acknowledged did believe in a supreme being) opted for 2. And 16.7% took the third vague alternative. The exact same study was repeated in 1996 by Larson and Witham and the results were unchanged. This means that over an 82 year period which has seen an

---

17. This is part of the wider 'Secularisation Thesis', the view that with the rise of modernity (which embraces industrialisation, urbanisation and rationalisation) there will be an inevitable corresponding decline in religion, resulting not only in the institutional separation of church and state and the reduction of the church's social power on society as a whole, but the decline of personal piety itself, i.e. religious belief will wither on the vine. See Melvin Tinker, 'Secularisation: Myth or Menace? An Assessment of Modern 'Worldliness'', *Themelios*, Vol 3, Issue 2, 2013.

accelerated modernization of society, there has been no decline even amongst the most liberal of beliefs.[18]

Also of significance is the Carnegie Commission's study of 1969 when 60,000 college professors were surveyed. This included questions such as 'What is your present religion?'; 'How religious do you consider yourself?' and 'Do you consider yourself religiously conservative?' Two striking findings came out which *challenged* the view that religion and science were incompatible. First, levels of religiousness were found to be relatively high. Second, the most religious (and most conservative) were to be found amongst the hard sciences—physics, chemistry etc. over and against the least religious being in the social sciences and psychology. Here we have highly intelligent and successful scientists who are more than comfortable with their religion and see no conflict between the two.

Just in case you think that I am being selective, let me quote Stephen Jay Gould, an atheist proponent of the theory of evolution. Responding to Dawkins he says, 'Either half my colleagues are enormously stupid, or else the science of Darwinism is fully compatible with conventional religious beliefs—and equally compatible with atheism.' That is, some Christians see the theory of evolution as being equivalent to the composition of the paper and ink content of Dr Pedant's letter—it is the *means* whereby God brought into being life.

---

18. Rodney Stark and Roger Finke, *Acts of Faith: Explaining the Human Side of Religion* (Berkeley: University of California Press, 2000), p. 73

From Material explanation to Biblical interpretation

So much for the book of nature which we need to read carefully to answer the 'how?' questions. But what of the 'why' questions? What is our purpose on earth if any? If there is a God, what is he like and how can we connect with him? To find the answers to those sorts of questions scientists like Francis Bacon, Galileo, Newton, Kepler, Faraday, Boyle and many others went to the other book, the Bible. Here we discover the infinite-personal God who moment by moment is intimately and passionately involved with that which he has made. He is the author of the whole show. What is more, he has made us primarily for relationships (Genesis 1:26ff). It is only by being rightly related to God that we find true value and significance. The problem is that we have turned our backs on him and broken that relationship (Genesis 3). Shakespeare as the author of *Hamlet* was 'outside' Hamlet's Denmark, but the Bible makes the amazing claim that some 2,000 years ago, God the author became a character in his creation, as the God incarnate Jesus of Nazareth. This is the way John describes this amazing event at the beginning of his biography of Jesus:

> In the beginning was the Word, and the Word was with God, and the Word was God. He was with God in the beginning. Through him all things were made; without him nothing was made that has been made. In him was life, and that life was the light of men … The Word became flesh and made his dwelling among us. We have seen his glory, the glory of the One and Only, who came from the Father, full of grace and truth. (John 1:1–14).

The Bible's claim is that through this person in some way

the world was originally made and furthermore he is its goal (*telos*), 'it was made by him and for him.' (Colossians 1:16). As a scientist would look carefully at the data and opt for the theory which best makes sense of it all, having what is called 'the best conceptual fit' so Christians invite others to look at the data of Jesus and decide for themselves.[19] But unlike obtaining scientific knowledge, which involves some degree of keeping a distance, this knowledge of God is more like having the personal knowledge of a friend, at some point you have to get close and make a commitment. Once that happens you start to see things differently through new eyes. You see yourself as someone precious in God's sight, having a clear purpose to know, love, serve and enjoy him—(even as a scientist maybe), together with a destination—to live with him for ever.

As mechanism and meaning are distinct and yet belong together as we look out on our world, so are science and Christianity.

---

19. 'Christian theology offers from its own distinctive point of view, a map of reality or "mask theory," which, though not exhaustive, is found to correspond to the observed features of nature. It makes possible a way of seeing things that is capable of accommodating the totality of human experience, and rendering it intelligible through its conceptual schemes', Alister E. McGrath, *Darwinism and the Divine* (Wiley-Blackwell, 2011), p 201

9

What is Sex for?

Introduction

For many years sociologists have spoken of the 'eroticization of Western Society'. That is to say that at almost every level we have simply become saturated with sex. 50 or so years ago the publication of D.H. Lawrence's novel, *Lady Chatterley's Lover* was sufficient to scandalize the nation into bringing about a court action to ban its publication. Now it appears on prime time TV and no one bats an eyelid. Similarly with advertising, we are told, 'sex sells'. Even government reports are required to be 'sexed up' at times.

Then there is the internet. In the United States pornography brings in more income than illicit drugs, alcohol and the entertainment industries *combined*. The internet hosts 420 million pages of pornographic material and 260 new porn sites are launched *every day*.[1]

---

1. http://www.techcrunch.com/2007/05/12/internet-pornography-stats/

This is our world—a world of sex.

In this chapter I want to take a step back so that we can think about the touchy topic of sex in the light of the Scriptures as a whole. This means that we will be getting to grips with some very important beliefs about sex—what it is and what it is for. Some reading this will be single, some engaged, some married, and some wrestling with aspects of our sexuality. Perhaps we may feel that we have 'got it together' in this area, that may be so, but *all* of us—if we are going to live God's way in God's world—do need to get these beliefs clear in our minds. To that end I will try and map out what the Bible has to say on the subject under three headings: Sex and the Big Picture; Sex and the Present World and Sex and the Redeemed Future.

Sex and the Big Picture

The fundamental question to be addressed is: what is sex for? You may think that the answer is obvious—it's for pleasure and procreation—having fun and making babies! That is not quite what I mean. From a *Biblical* standpoint, considered within the wider perspective of God's purpose for the world, what is sex for?

Perhaps we can get more easily to the answer if we ask the bigger question of which this is just a part: what is *anything* for? The apostle Paul in Romans 14:7 tells us: 'None of us lives for himself alone and none of us dies to himself alone. If we live, we live to the Lord; and if we die, we die to the Lord. So whether we live or die, we belong to the Lord. For this very reason, Christ dies and returned to life so that he might be Lord of both the dead and the living.' Life and existence and everything that goes to make up that has to do with 'living unto the Lord'. And so in the section on sex which Paul penned in 1 Corinthians 6, he concludes his treatment with these words: 'Therefore, *honour* God with your body.' So it is all to do with honouring, glorifying, doing things unto the Lord—that is what sex is for. The question is: how?

To answer that question we need to go back to God's design plan for creation.

Sometimes when discussing matters of sexuality, for instance the issue of homosexuality, the objection is raised by the one with same sex-attraction; 'But this is normal for me, this is who I am' as if that settles the matter. But to say that something is *normal* is not the same thing as saying it is *proper*. To claim something is acting normally is a matter of statistics, to say something is acting properly is a matter of design plan and purpose. For example, I might say that my car is acting normally when it requires three turns of the ignition key to get it going—that is normal for my car. But that is not what the manufacturer had in mind when the car was designed; it is simply not acting *properly*. But in order to know what is the proper way men and women are to express their sexuality we have to have access to the great Designer's plan. And that, of course, is what the Bible provides.

This is expressed in a variety of ways including the fact that the world is built according to *wisdom*—Proverbs 3:19, 'The LORD by wisdom founded the earth; by understanding he established the heavens.' When God brought the universe into being, he did so according to the blueprint called 'wisdom'. In other words, the world is constructed in a particular way to achieve certain ends intended by the Maker.

This not only includes the material order of the universe but the moral order too. To go with the flow of wisdom, the way God made things and intended things to run is not inhibiting, it is freedom. It is when we run counter to that, as when a man decides to throw away the instruction manual to a sophisticated hi fi system and decides to go it alone, that one is inviting trouble. As Oliver O'Donovan writes, Creation Order is 'not negotiable within the course of history' and is part of 'that which neither the terrors of chance nor the ingenuity of art can overthrow. It defines the scope of our freedom and the limits of our fears.'[2] Similarly Kevin Vanhoozer:

> Genesis gives what we might call the 'design plan' for sexuality. It explains how sexuality is supposed to function. The activities of our bodies must fit the way we were made. This is not merely an argument from biology to morality. On the contrary, the Bible views biology and morality together, just as it views body and soul together. We are not simply neutral sexual beings, but male and female, and we honour God when we honour our male-female complementarity. Men and women are made to find sexual fulfilment with each other.[3]

Foundational to our understanding of God's purpose in sex, according to both Jesus and Paul,[4] is Genesis 2:24, "For this reason a man will leave his father and mother and be united to his wife, and they will become one flesh"

---

2. Oliver O'Donovan, *Resurrection and Moral Order* (Eerdmans, 1994), p 61

3. Kevin Vanhoozer, 'The Bible—its Relevance Today' in *God, Family and Sexuality* ed. David W. Torrance (Handsel Press, 1997), p 27

4. Matthew 19:5; Ephesians 5:31

In theory God could have chosen all sorts of ways to ensure the propagation of the human species, but the implication here is that he created us as *sexual* beings whose sexuality is to be expressed only in the exclusive, permanent, social, and sexual union of one man with one woman, publicly pledged and recognized by society in what is called marriage. Implicit within this idea of 'leaving and cleaving' is that of making a promise. The Bible's word for this is *covenant*, which is the background to another key passage—Malachi 2:14, 'The Lord is acting as the witness between you and the wife of your youth ... she is your partner, the wife of your marriage *covenant*.' This idea might contrast to this verse written in a Hallmark card: 'I can't promise forever. But I can promise you today.' What we have in those two contrasting statements are two mutually exclusive views of love. There is Hallmark love, the love of the 21st century, which is unsure, ephemeral, here today and who knows about tomorrow? It is a love which breeds insecurity for it places us at the mercy of the emotional highs or lows of the other person—people fall in love and they fall out of love. Not so the love of the wedding service. When the groom and bride say 'I will' to each other, they don't mean 'I think you are the best-looking babe or the beefiest hunk in the whole wide world!' They are not so much paying the other person a compliment as making a personal commitment—'I will be true to you'. It is within the security of *that* relationship, publically pledged and publically acknowledged that sex is to take place.

Going back to Genesis we need to place the verse about male and female becoming one flesh in its wider setting if we are going to really understand what sex is for.

The context is set for us by Genesis 1:27–31, where human beings are presented as the pinnacle of God's act of creation being made as male and female in his image who are blessed and commanded to be ... fruitful and increase in number. Why? So that they can fill the earth, bring it under control and rule over everything under God. *How* we are made—in 'God's image'—'male and female'—is linked to what we were made *for*—to rule the earth. This is the way Christopher Ash helpfully puts it:

> Human sexuality is to be understood within this matrix of meaning, encompassing human dignity (in the image of God) and human task (exercising dominion). Within the Order of Creation, humankind is placed uniquely with a dual orientation. On the one hand, towards the Creator, humankind is given moral responsibility; on the other, towards creation, they are entrusted with a task. Holding these together is the key to the purpose of sex.[5]

We are now much closer to answering the question: 'Why sex?'

In Genesis 1 with the climax of the Sabbath day when God is pleased with what he has made we are pointed in the direction of why there is *anything* at all. John Calvin sums up the purpose like this: 'After the world was created, man was placed in it as in a theatre, that he, beholding above him and beneath the wonderful works of God, might reverently

---

adore their Author'.[6] In other words, the whole of creation is the arena of God's glory and everything in it is meant to reflect back to him that glory in praise—including sex. On the more general point, John Piper writes: 'The created universe is all about glory. The deepest longing of the human heart and the deepest meaning of heaven and earth are summed up in this: the glory of God. The universe was made to show it, and we were made to see it and savour it. Nothing less will do.'[7] Therefore, sex somehow is meant to show God's glory and in it we are to *savour* his glory. How might this be so? Let's turn again to Genesis 2 and verse 18.

This section of Genesis begins with a portrait of a world that is badly in need of a gardener: 'there was no human being to work the ground'(2:6). God makes Adam in (2:7) because the world needs a gardener, namely, someone to steward and care for it. The general picture we have of man in the park is of a Priest-King. He is a King who is to rule his little domain. But he is also a priest in that his work in the divine sanctuary of the garden is meant to be an act of worship. And it is in *this* setting we are told in verse 18 that God said, 'It is not good for the man to be alone.' The natural reading is not that Adam experienced relational loneliness, although that may well be there too, but rather that he had been entrusted with a task that was too big for him to do all by himself. And so God goes on to say, 'I will make a helper.' The term 'helper'[8] doesn't mean skivvy. It implies someone who assists and encourages

---

6. John Calvin, *Institutes of the Christian Religion*, tr. Henry Beveridge, Eerdmans, 1998, 1.14.20.

7. John Piper, *Seeing and Savouring Jesus Christ* (IVP, 2001), p 13.

8. '*ezer*'

making up for something which is lacking. God in Scripture is described as a helper.[9] It also carries the idea of a helper matching man's eminence (the qualifying term *kenegdo* meaning this helper is "fit" for the man). It is therefore a position of great standing and privilege.

This raises the question: in what way will the woman help with the task? Genesis 2 doesn't specifically tell us. But it is natural to include the procreation and nurture of children, which has been underscored in Genesis 1 where humankind has been given the blessing and exhortation to 'be fruitful and multiply, fill the earth and subdue it.' So presumably one way the woman helps the man is by enabling the procreation, birth, and nurture of children. Not only is the park too big for Adam to look after on his own; it is too big for Adam *and* Eve to look after solely by themselves—let alone the rest of the earth!

Genesis 1 and 2 suggest to us that both the procreational and the relational purposes of sex come under the wider purpose of serving God by caring for his world. There is certainly delight and intimacy in Genesis 2:32. Here is a natural and innocent affirmation of sexual desire and delight, of nakedness untouched by shame. But this delight is not an end in itself. On the contrary, here is delight with a shared purpose, intimacy with a common goal, and companionship in a task that expands beyond the boundaries of the couple's relationship on its own. As we rejoice with the lovers in the garden, we must not forget that there is work to be done. The garden needs tilling, weeding, watching. The purpose of sex is not

9. Psalm 33:20

ultimately their mutual delight, wonderful though that is. It is that the woman should be just the helper the man needs so that together they may serve and watch the garden.[10]

I would wish to extend this further by saying it is in serving God this way that we glorify God and so fulfil our reason for our being on earth.

More specifically let us ask: how might sex serve and glorify God?

One way, as we have seen, is by having children and nurturing them in the knowledge of God so that they can serve him too. This means not only using whatever gifts they have where God has placed them in his providence, but this side of the fall, proclaiming the Gospel so that God's original intention of having the earth filled and subdued will be achieved through people coming under the Lordship of his Son.

Secondly, sex has a bonding effect between husband and wife and is part of the nurturing of each other in togetherness, so that in the 'theatre of God's glory' they will function well together and so display before the world God's intention for a good marriage. This is implied in the 'cleaving.' In the Greek translation of the Old Testament (LXX) a word is used normally meaning 'glue'. Well-functioning couples serving the Lord are a good thing and good sex helps with that.

Thirdly, God is served and so glorified in sex in that it acts as a mirror to the world of the relationship between God

---

10. Christopher Ash, op cit.

and his people—'as the bridegroom rejoices over the bride, so shall your God rejoice over you' (Isaiah 62:5), 'For this reason a man will leave his father and mother and the two will become one flesh. This is a profound mystery—but I am talking about Christ and the church.' (Ephesians 5:31-32).

The faithful love of husband and wife serves God by providing in this world a visible image of the love God has for his people and their answering love. God wants this kind of relationship to display one of the ways in which the invisible God becomes visible in his world. When a couple devotes time and energy to nurturing their own love for each other, paradoxically they may also be serving God, if they love one another with the longing that their love will begin to approximate the love between God and his people.[11]

Or put to the matter in terms of biblical theology, the world was created so that 'the eternal Son of God might obtain a spouse'.[12]

In summary, the way God has designed and set things up in terms of creation, both material and moral, is linked to the purpose he intends, namely, procreation, nurturing, praise and declaring the Gospel.

Sex in the Present World
That was God's design plan, but that is not the way it operates at present. In Romans 8:20, the apostle Paul tells us that

---

11. Christopher Ash, op cit.

12. Jonathan Edwards, 'The Church's Marriage to Her Sons, and to her God.' In Sermons and Discourses, 1743-1758, vol 25 of *The Works of Jonathan Edwards* (Yale University Press, 206), p 187

the whole of creation was subject to *frustration* by God, but in hope that the creation will one day be liberated from its bondage to decay and brought into the glorious freedom of the sons of God (vv 20–21).[13] In other words, Creation is no longer *ordered* according to God's good design, it is *disordered* due to sin. This includes sex.

Frustration in sex occurs at a number of different levels and in a number of different ways.

There may be a long period before marriage—that can be frustrating. Some people never marry. Others are widowed young. Many experience same-sex desires for a while, and for some these same-sex desires intensify and stay with them for a long time, maybe a lifetime. Most people experience sexual desire towards not one, but many other people. Married people experience frustrations and disappointments in the sexual intimacy of their marriage relationships through physical and mental illness. Even those whose sexual relationships are mostly satisfying and on the whole God-honouring will nonetheless experience adulterous or pornographic desires. Some who wish to have children will find those desires frustrated by involuntary childlessness. Others have children, but the children get ill and die, or the children disappoint by rebelling against Christ. In so many different ways sexual disorder appears within and amongst us all.

One of the greatest pressures is substituting sex for God.

---

13. 'Futility'—*mataiotes* is the same word used by the Greek translation of the Bible known as the Septuagint (LXX) to translate *hebel* 'meaninglessness' in Ecclesiastes

This is not surprising given the close link between God's intentions and sex, but it is disastrous nonetheless. One author writes, 'It is an ironic thought that just at the moment when some thinkers are heralding the advent of the perfect marriage based on full satisfaction of the sexual, emotional and creative needs of both husband and wife, the proportion of marital breakdowns ... is rising rapidly'.[14] This is because sex is being expected to bear a weight it was never meant to bear, in other words, it has become idolatrous.

To a greater or lesser extent we *all* have disordered sexual desires; the first step is recognizing them as such and then to admit we all have problems.

The second step is to hold on to the doctrine of Creation in which God as the Sovereign Creator also enables a Christian to believe that in his Providence the state I find myself in at the moment—maybe single, perhaps married to an unresponsive spouse or whatever it may be, is no accident. God still reigns, he still cares and we are called to trust and obey.

Thirdly, we believe that the Gospel is good news of real *change,*

> The grace of God teaches us to say 'No' to ungodliness and worldly passions, and to live self-controlled, upright and godly lives in this present age, while we wait for the blessed hope—the glorious appearing of our great God and Saviour, Jesus Christ, who gave himself for us to redeem us from all

---

14. L. Stone, *'The Family, Sex and Marriage in England, 1500–1800'* (London: Pelican, 1979), p 427.

wickedness and to purify for himself a people that are his very own, eager to do what is good (Titus 2:12–14).

There is no promise that this will necessarily be an easy process in the area of our sexuality than in any other area of our fallen nature, but the promise is there and that is why we need to be part of a fellowship whereby we can help each other and hold each other accountable as we are filled with God's Spirit.

Sex and the redeemed future

Christians are always looking to the future. They know that this world with its mix of the good, the bad and the ugly, even in the arena of sex, is not all that there is or will be: the best is yet to come. The *whole* of creation, including the sexual element, is 'groaning as in the pains of childbirth' [here is an interesting sexual metaphor!] right up to the present time says Paul (Romans 8:22). But Christians are people of hope as they look to a glorious future—their liberation, including, if you will, a sexual liberation. Even back in Genesis 2 with the garden and the wedding, within the full sweep of Scripture we are being pointed forward to another garden and another wedding indeed, another priest-king who seeks out his bride. That garden is Gethsemane; the Priest-King is Jesus who offered his whole being as a sacrifice—a sacrifice which was to be completed on a hill—Golgotha. It was there out of his wounded side that God brought forth his bride—the Church. All that we need, he has promised to provide, for if we are trusting in Christ, *we* are *his* 'bone of his bone and flesh of his flesh' loved with an everlasting love (Ephesians 5:22–33). The church is his glory and that which God had purposed from eternity will be fulfilled—the dwelling of God with his people—Revelation 21:1 'Then I saw a new heaven and a new earth, for the first heaven and the first earth had passed away, and there was no longer any sea. I saw the Holy City, the New Jerusalem, coming down out of heaven from God, prepared as a bride beautifully dressed for her husband.' As the bride on her wedding day shares the glory of her husband, the church shares the glory of her Saviour. All the passion and intensity of love which we see portrayed, for example in the Song of Songs, will be surpassed when Christian believers as the Bride of Christ encounter the bridegroom on that great day.

John Piper is quite explicit about the role sex has in pointing us towards this: 'Just as the heavens are telling the glory of God's power and beauty, so sexual climax is telling the glory of immeasurable delights that we will have with Christ in the age to come. There will be no marriage there. But what marriage meant will be there. And the pleasures of marriage, ten-to-the-millionth power, will be there.'[15]

---

15. John Piper, *This Momentary Marriage—A Parable of Permanence* (Inter Varsity Press, 2009), p 128

10

When does Tolerance become Tyranny?

Introduction

No one likes to be accused of being intolerant. To be branded as intolerant puts you in the same category as a fascist, a bigot, someone who is subversive of democracy. Tolerance has been elevated to the status of the ultimate virtue alongside what might be thought of as the eleventh commandment, 'Thou shalt not offend'. This has led to an interesting paradox: as a society we can be tolerant of anything but intolerance. We must be 'intolerant of intolerance' (so asserted former British Prime Minister, David Cameron).

Words, words, words

Such a view is both right and wrong.

It all depends upon what we mean by the word 'tolerance.'

Until relatively recently 'tolerance' was simply taken as the need for a society to allow people to practice and promote their own beliefs without fear or favour. After years of in-fighting between different branches of the Christian church following the Reformation in the 16th century, Europe eventually adopted a policy of toleration. In Britain the Act of Toleration (1689) was a major landmark. Thinkers like Roger Williams in America and John Owen in Britain believed that religious conflict (by which they meant conflict between Christians), did not serve the cause of Christ. Tolerance for them was a virtue born of confidence in the ability of the Truth to vindicate itself without the state needing to resort to force.

Put simply, the way folk operated with this understanding of tolerance meant that whilst I may not subscribe to your beliefs and would hold views entirely different and opposed to your own, nonetheless I would fight for your right to hold the views you do hold.[1] There are two things of note here. The right to believe does not mean that all beliefs are right. Here we are speaking about the right to *believing*, which should be protected. It does not extend to protecting *beliefs*—such as, for example, Sharia law. Secondly, this stance at least presupposes that there is something called 'Truth' over which people were disagreeing.

Change of meaning

By and large that is no longer the case because the very idea of 'tolerance' has been drastically altered.[2] Whilst in the past, to a greater or lesser extent, we lived in a pluralist society—

---

1. This has been attributed to Voltaire

2. For a thorough discussion of this issue see, D. A. Carson, *Christ and Culture Revisited* (Nottingham: Apollos, 2008).

that is, a society made up of a variety of beliefs which could be discussed and argued about while (hopefully) showing respect *but* still believing they can't all be valid—the shift is now towards pluralis*m*. This is the idea that all views are of equal worth. We are not dealing with facts, so it is claimed, but beliefs, and since beliefs are personal (with the accompanying idea that they are private and even subjective), they should not be allowed to venture out into the public domain for that is when they are liable to become socially disruptive.

What matters in the popular mind at least is the *positive* notion of sincerity. As long as a person is sincere in their beliefs—live and let live. This is accompanied with an underlying *negative* assumption that people have a right not to be offended. What is more, to claim that one belief is right and others are wrong smacks of arrogance—a kind of intellectual imperialism. All of this is related to the shift that has taken place in the West with regards to an understanding of truth which has been relativised. Truth, like beauty, is very much in the eye of the beholder. This lies at the heart of postmodernism. Here the question is no longer, 'Is it true?' But, '*Whose* truth is it?' This is illustrated by an article in a best-selling magazine in Britain which I was reading not too long ago which included this little piece of advice given by Damien Barr for those who wish to write their memoir, 'Too many facts can get in the way of truth. *The truth is what you feel*; the facts are what you know and can argue about'.[3] Pluralism and relativism, and indeed, subjectivism, are closely intertwined.

---

3. Quoted in 'How to Write your Memoir' SAGA April 2016 p59

Sociological and philosophical pluralism

Here we need to make an important distinction between *sociological pluralism* on the one hand and *philosophical pluralism* on the other. Sociological pluralism simply recognises a diversity of beliefs and practices. Different people dress in different ways, have different languages, accents, different cuisine and so on and so forth. I happen to like Chinese food, others prefer Tex Mex. We are not necessarily worse off for having these different cultures living side by side and intermixing in a modern Western society, on the contrary, a good case could be made that it is enriching in so many ways. That is simply a fact of the way things *are*.

Philosophical pluralism is a different thing entirely (although it tends to be parasitic on the former). According to this view, to claim that one religion is better than another is inherently *wrong*. Beliefs, like moral values, are relative. The pressure then begins to mount that in order to make sure that we have a tolerant society (that is, according to the 'new' tolerance) those who do not buy into this belief cannot be tolerated and must be made to see the error of their ways and, if necessary, silenced.

Putting it simply: sociological pluralism is descriptive—describing how things are; philosophical pluralism is prescriptive, declaring how things should be.[4]

---

4. D.A. Carson notes that there is a further modification of what we have described as sociological pluralism (he prefers the term 'empirical pluralism'), namely 'cherished pluralism'. Here empirical pluralism is considered to be something valuable, and so to be cherished, in itself. This then forms the stepping stone to making philosophical pluralism plausible, indeed, appearing to be logical. See D. A. Carson, *'The Gagging of God'* (Apollos, 1996), pp. 13–21

It might be worth highlighting at this point whether it is desirable to use the term 'tolerance' at all, even the old style tolerance for a very fundamental reason, viz., the word 'tolerance' contains within it a 'power equation'; the strong tolerating the weak, the clever tolerating the not so clever, the majority tolerating the minority, the government tolerating the citizens and so on. The word which might come closer to encapsulating that which is desirable and is more in line with the tolerance of John Locke and others might be 'respect'. Whatever our standing in relation to others, we accord respect for their basic rights, traditionally construed in terms of the right to freedom of conscience (believing), freedom of expression and freedom of assembly.

Examples of intolerant tolerance

We are not dealing here with abstract ideas, for a seismic shift in our culture has taken place having profound effects in every strata of society. Let me mention a few examples of the way the new intolerant tolerance is working itself out.

In 2005, Noah Riner, then President of the Dartmouth Student assembly addressed a convocation welcoming freshmen to the campus. He spoke of education being more than acquiring information; it also involved the development of character. Much of this, he said, came through self-sacrifice and 'the best example of this is Jesus ... he knew the right thing to do.' He then briefly spoke about what Jesus achieved on the cross. Controversy ensued and the vice-president of the student body wrote to him complaining that his choice of topic was 'reprehensible and an abuse of power'. Reflecting on this Riner insightfully observed that it was not the case that Dartmouth had a speech *code*, which would be easy to deal with, but a speech *culture,* such that some topics are not only off limits but can't be uttered.[5]

Another example comes from Brown University during the Gulf War. Some students decided to fly American flags outside their dorm windows to show support for the troops fighting in the Persian Gulf. Subsequently the university authorities asked for the flags to be removed for no other reason that the practice might offend other students who did not support the war.[6]

Here is an example from Great Britain: 'When Patricia Gearing's daughter died of Batten's Disease in 1998, her grave was marked by a simple cross. Before long Mrs. Gearing was instructed by the local authority to remove it. Their rules said, 'Crosses are discouraged as excessive use of the supreme Christian symbol is undesirable.' The family was given permission to erect a headstone featuring Mickey Mouse instead.'[7]

Keep your beliefs to yourself

One of the results of this change is the *privatisation of convictions.* Under the new order we can hold whatever convictions we like so long as we don't express them. Or rather, there *are* convictions which are allowed to be expressed and *only* expressed, and that is the conviction that all views are valid and it is not proper to question other

---

5. Cited in D.A. Carson's *The Intolerance of Tolerance* (Inter Varsity Press, 2012), pp 29–30

6. Cited by S. D. Gaede, op cit., p 22

7. *The Times,* 6 September 1998

people's beliefs and behaviour—*except* those who believe you should question beliefs and behaviour!

In a nutshell, the traditional view of tolerance which nurtured freedom of thought and speech in the West for centuries, enabling people to get alongside each other albeit not without difficulty in some cases, was the view that the *person* whose views are different should be tolerated or respected, unless they threatened the well-being of society; the new toleration insists that it is the *views* which are to be tolerated and more than that, 'celebrated'.

Let is consider how this new toleration is being enforced almost unconsciously in the sense that living in a modern world makes it seem not only plausible but *desirable*—even for professing Christians. In other words, at the level of our *gut* reactions, many of us are finding ourselves being lured to becoming relativists.

The Reinforcers

First, there is an increased awareness of other beliefs in all their bewildering variety. This is what I call the 'supermarket effect'.[8] Think of what happens when you go into a mega store to buy, say, a tube of toothpaste. I guess, for guys toothpaste is toothpaste—what the heck. But that just adds to the bewilderment when the poor fellow is standing there

---

8. Peter Berger in his book *The Heretical Imperative* (Doubleday, 1980), argues that the idea of a free market monopolises the Western scene. He points out that the word 'heresy' originally derives from the Greek verb '*haireo*' meaning 'I choose'. A heretic is literally a person who chooses what he wants to believe. In this sense, he claims, all modern people are forced to be heretics by the pluralistic supermarket in which they now live.

with rows and rows of the stuff—how do you choose between them? You have minty flavour, strawberry flavour, toothpaste with whitener, toothpaste with extra fluoride and so on. One response is to say: 'It's just a matter of personal preference—whatever works for you.' The temptation is then to think: it is all relative, sure, there may be one or two differences, but they are more or less all the same—after all, toothpaste is toothpaste.

That same supermarket effect can spill over into the way we approach other faiths and ideas. Is it really the case that one belief is just as good as another—beneath they are all the same but just packaged differently? Is it simply a question of personal preference? It may certainly *feel* like that at times.

Think too of the experience of many students. This is helpfully sketched out by Stanley Gaede:

'Consider' he writes:

> The day of a typical university student—let's call him Steve. At 8.00 he takes a shower while talking to his roommate about the keg party the night before. At 8.30 he has breakfast with a Hare Krishna devotee who not only didn't attend the party but doesn't even drink Coke. At 9.00 he attends an ecology class where the predominant assumption is that humankind and nature are one. Later in the library, he begins work on a research paper exploring a neo-Marxist interpretation of the fall of the Soviet empire; afterwards he meets his girlfriend for lunch and conversation, the overriding theme of which is how the two feel about one another. In the afternoon he attends a lecture on microeconomics that offers an entirely different interpretation of the Soviet collapse; this is followed by a quick

dash to the lounge so he can catch another instalment of As the World Turns.[9]

The point is, modern students, and much of the rest of us, find ourselves swept into a wide variety of discrete frames of reference. There is a constant switching from one way of thinking to another. This not only adds to the *feeling* that everything is relative—different views are, well, just different views—but it makes it difficult to have any integrity, that is, a frame of reference which *integrates* these different experiences in a meaningful way. The result is that we can undergo a kind of 'cognitive dissonance', a feeling of mental dislocation—especially for the Christian. So on Sunday night in the 'world of church' the Christian is singing 'Jesus is Lord', but on Monday morning out in the 'real world' of cut and thrust business or lectures, there are many 'lords' to contend with. And so the temptation to 'go with the flow' and separate off our religious life from our intellectual life, moral life, and social life thus buying in to the new tolerance will be almost irresistible.

Secondly, our modern view of freedom enforces the new view of toleration. For the ancients it mattered *what* we chose. For the moderns it is *that* we choose. The ability to make choices we see as expressing our freedom. And not surprisingly the more we can choose from, the more we think we are free and so significant. Descartes' *'Cogito ergo sum'* 'I think therefore I am' has been transmuted into *'Volo ergo sum'*—'I *choose* therefore I am'. We can therefore

9. S.D. Gaede, *When Tolerance is No Virtue: Political Correctness, Multiculturalism and the Future of Truth and Justice* (InterVarsity Press, Downers Grove, Illinois), 1993, p 57

understand how this moves into the question of gender. Some, like feminist Judith Butler[10] argue that gender is a social construct not a biological 'given' and so the ultimate choice is of our gender, hence the perceived right for people to be transgender, stating their preferred gender regardless of their biological sex. We therefore not only have *lifestyle* choices, but *life meaning* choices which enhances our feeling of self-esteem even further. Meaning to life is not given to us by God, but chosen by *us*!

A Christian perspective

Let's look at the issue of pluralism and the new tolerance a little more closely from a Christian perspective.

First, pluralism in the sense that a variety of beliefs and practices exist side by side is nothing new. Old Testament Israel was born into a pluralistic world. As they entered the Promised Land, Israel was surrounded by a bewildering array of beliefs and practices vying for their allegiance. Accordingly the Israelites were confronted with the religions and rituals of the Canaanites, Hittites, Moabites, and Hivites. But they were quite clear in their understanding that the God of the universe, who had revealed himself to them, forbade them adopting the beliefs of these other peoples. However sincere the worshippers of the god Molech were, the Jews were not to tolerate the sacrifice of children to such idols by burning them alive. But according to the modern day pluralist, the Jews should have simply recognised that baby burning was different, not wrong.

---

10. See Gabriele Kuby, *The Global Sexual Revolution* (Angelico Press, 2012), pp 44–48

Secondly, the early Christians went even further. Most of them were Jews but said that the God of the Old Testament had come into history in the form of the carpenter from Nazareth. This was not a myth, nor an idea, but a matter of historical fact on the same level as Julius Caesar crossing the Rubicon. They had met him, heard him and touched him— as the apostle John writes (1 John 1:1). They were, as it were, *forced* to believe and teach this, not out of fear, but out of conviction. They were compelled not by fanaticism but by the facts. They could no more deny that Jesus is Lord and Saviour than Galileo could deny that the earth revolved around the sun. Here the Christians went against the political correctness of their age. This was the time of the Roman Empire. Edward Gibbon describes the religious scene in this way: 'The various modes of worship which prevailed in the Roman world were all considered by the people as equally true, by the philosophers as equally false, and by the magistrates as equally useful.' The Romans had no difficulty in adding a new god to their list, but the Christians said there is only One God and he can only be known through Jesus. The result was that they were not tolerated but tortured.

This leads on to the main reason why this view of pluralism and the new tolerance is quite intolerable, because at the end of the day it is harmful to the issue of truth and so a threat to toleration itself.

The Flat earth conundrum

Let me illustrate this by telling you of the experience of a friend of mine.[11]

---

11. Phillip P Jensen, 'The Tyranny of Tolerance,' *The Briefing*, Issue 50, 1990

My friend went to a meeting of the Flat Earth Society. The friend said there was one speaker there. He seemed sincere. He looked sincere. He acted sincere. But my friend, who is a Christian, thought that the speaker's facts were plain wrong. The observer admitted this was intolerant of him. Maybe the speaker wasn't wrong. Maybe, if the advocate of the flat earth theory was as sincere as he looked, he was right. Perhaps the crowd was wrong, although they looked sincere too. Perhaps they were both right. Maybe the earth was flat for the speaker and round for crowd and just confusing for my friend. But of course if that were the case then things would keep on changing. They would keep moving from the world being flat to being round to being flat again depending upon what a person believed at the time, provided, of course, the person believed sincerely.

But the odd thing was that the crowd was not very tolerant of the little man from the Flat earth society. They did not listen to his arguments. They jeered him, as, no doubt, in the same way people jeered at Galileo and Copernicus for arguing in the opposite direction. Naturally they were intolerant of him, because he was being intolerant of them for he was claiming to be right. If only he had been claiming that people can believe nothing or everything about the world, then he might have been given an easier ride. But I doubt that would have been acceptable either. The world is either flat or round and it cannot be both.

This is the tyranny of relativism which masquerades as tolerance, because it soon becomes intolerant. Some people, let alone their views are *not* to be respected.

This is often the case with people's attitude towards Christians.

'So you believe in God? Well, some people do, some people don't.'

'You are sincere. I am sincere. Your god helps you, fine, my non-god helps me. Let's live together in tolerance.'

But of course such tolerance is false. It is not simply disagreeing to disagree and still getting on with each other. It is saying that when it comes to certain things, *truth does not matter*. The move from the belief that truth does not matter to *forcing* people to agree that truth does not matter is but a small one. What do you do with someone like the Christian who makes the sort of claim that as a matter of fact Jesus is or is not God incarnate? Or that He did or did not rise from the dead. He could not have remained dead and risen from the dead at the same time—that is nonsense. We may disagree about the facts and still continue to live in the same society. That would be what J. Budziszewski calls 'true tolerance'. But to accept each other's beliefs based upon both being right when we are clearly contradicting each other is intolerable—for it comes at too high a price—the price of truth. But for the sake of promoting a certain view of tolerance—which involves relativising all beliefs—that is when persecution is just around the corner. And of course that is what happened in a society similar to ours—1st Century Rome.

Here are some words of the 19th century British Prime Minister, William Gladstone: Rome, the mistress of state-craft, and beyond all other nations in the political employment of religion, added without stint or scruple to her list of gods and goddesses, and consolidated her military empire by the skilful medley of all the religions of the world. Thus it continued while the worship of the Deity was but a conjecture or a contrivance; but when the rising Sun of Righteousness had given reality to the subjective forms of faith, and had made actual and solid truth the common inheritance of all men, the religion of Christ became, unlike other new creeds, an object of jealousy and of cruel persecution, because it would not consent to become a partner in the heterogeneous device, and planted itself upon the truth and not in the quicksand of opinion ... Should the Christian faith ever become but one among many co-equal pensioners of a government, it will be proof that subjective religion has again lost its God-given hold upon objective reality; or when, under the thin shelter of its name, a multitude of discordant schemes shall have put upon a footing of essential parity, and shall together receive the bounty of legislature, this will prove that we are once more in a transition state—that we are travelling back again from the region to which the Gospel brought us to that in which it found us.

In other words, if the pursuit of tolerance in society results in the general erosion of the public confidence in objective Truth, then pluralism will not lead to a neutral secular society on matters of religion, but an anti-Christian, pagan one like ancient Rome. Pluralism will only tolerate pluralists and will not look kindly on those who believe in Truth with a capital 'T'. What those who blindly go along with the new tolerance fail to see is that it is objective truth which preserves all freedoms. If it is a matter of mere relativism on questions of belief and morality, then argumentation and rational persuasion will have no place and then it will be left to those with the loudest voices or the greatest political clout to ensure they get their own way. The way of persuasion will be overtaken by coercion. This we see happening today in Western Europe and the United States.

A biblical basis for toleration

Is there a Biblical basis for true toleration—extending to others the respect to basic rights we would wish others to extend to us? Indeed there is and it rests upon four fundamental pillars.

• The nature of human beings

Scripture presents human beings as those who make significant choices which entail personal responsibility. To reduce this capacity in a person either by political or religious coercion or technological or social manipulation is to make a person less than God has made them to be. Since God relates to Adam as a responsible moral agent in the Garden of Eden by bestowing upon him, in the words of Pascal, the 'dignity of causality,' Christians and all people of good will should seek to uphold, protect and enhance this aspect of a person's being as one made in God's image. The literary critic George Steiner wrote, 'More than *Homo sapiens*, we are *Homo quaerens*, the animal that asks and asks.' This is an expression of people being made in the image of God and so any move to prevent questions being thought or asked, even under the guise of tolerance, should firmly be resisted.

• The nature of the Biblical ethic

To go no further than the second great commandment to 'love your neighbour as yourself' (Mark 12:31) and the golden rule, 'Do to others as you would have them do to you' (Luke 6:31) we have a significant ethical motive in promoting true toleration. It is out of neighbourly love that we would wish people to exercise their God-given capacities to think and decide what they should believe and how they should express those beliefs. This command also provides the boundary limit for toleration, the fence around the playground of ideas so that within those boundaries we may play at liberty and safely. The love of neighbour would forbid oppression and victimisation as well as those practices which aim at the impoverishment and destruction of our neighbour, for example when people are threatened with violence—physical or verbal. The golden rule captures the moral direction in which we are to move. Christians would desire that members of other faiths and non-faiths extend to us the freedom to worship as we wish and to promote our religious views by the same token Christians must insist that the same courtesy is extended to them. This is showing genuine respect.

• The nature of the Gospel

The Gospel is news of what God has done in Jesus Christ which calls for a response of repentance and trust. Whilst affirming the enabling work of the Holy Spirit in the act of regeneration (John 3: 3) this does not entail coercion. The Gospel itself attests to the freedom and responsibility of human beings before their Maker and is itself a means of bringing about true freedom—freedom from the curse of the law (Galatians 4) and a freedom to act in ways we were designed to think and act by keeping in step with the Spirit (Galatians 5).

- **The nature of the Kingdom of God.**
If the kingdom of God were to be identified with an earthly institution, then it is a short step to implementing earthly means to establish it. This was the folly of the crusades and the persecution of free churchman in the seventeenth century by the established church in Britain. Paul insists that the weapons we use are not the 'weapons of this world' (2 Corinthians 10:4). This is a kingdom which is truly *inclusive* 'There is neither Jew nor Gentile, neither slave nor free, nor is there male and female, for you are all one in Christ Jesus' (Galatians 3:28) and as Christians we are to seek to display that in the kingdom's outposts, namely the local churches.

Conclusion
As Jesus did not repay evil for evil, but set forth the way of the cross where strength is seen in weakness; that is the way we his followers are to travel. As citizens of a democratic society we are free (some would argue, obligated), to use all legitimate means at our disposal to argue, persuade and change views and opinions, not in order to 'impose' our beliefs, but to *work out* those beliefs in a way, we think will best benefit our neighbour and honour God. But, if we follow the way of the cross, then the road we tread may be a painful road, one of rejection and abuse.

The call for the church in the secularised West to be prepared to suffer (and we must all face this possibility) also rounds off D. A. Carson's treatment of the corrosive effect of secularisation in producing a more intolerant society. But he also offers these words of encouragement with which I would like to conclude:

Delight in God, and trust in him. God remains sovereign, wise and good. Our ultimate confidence is not in any government or party, still less in our ability to mould the culture in which we live.[12]

---

12. Carson, *The Intolerance of Tolerance*, p 176